Tucholsky Wagner Zola Scott Sydow Freud Schlegel
Turgenev Wallace Fonatne
Twain Walther von der Vogelweide Fouqué Friedrich II. von Preußen
Weber Freiligrath Frey
Kant Ernst
Fechner Weiße Rose von Fallersleben Richthofen Frommel
Fichte Hölderlin
Engels Fielding Eichendorff Tacitus Dumas
Fehrs Faber Flaubert Eliasberg Ebner Eschenbach
Feuerbach Maximilian I. von Habsburg Fock Zweig
Ewald Eliot Vergil
Goethe Elisabeth von Österreich London
Mendelssohn Balzac Shakespeare Dostojewski Ganghofer
Lichtenberg Rathenau Doyle Gjellerup
Trackl Stevenson Hambruch
Mommsen Tolstoi Lenz Droste-Hülshoff
Thoma Hanrieder
Dach Verne von Arnim Hägele Hauff Humboldt
Reuter Rousseau Hagen Hauptmann Gautier
Karrillon Garschin Baudelaire
Damaschke Defoe Hebbel
Descartes Hegel Kussmaul Herder
Wolfram von Eschenbach Dickens Schopenhauer Rilke George
Bronner Darwin Melville Grimm Jerome Bebel Proust
Campe Horváth Aristoteles Voltaire Federer
Bismarck Vigny Barlach Herodot
Gengenbach Heine
Storm Casanova Tersteegen Grillparzer Georgy
Chamberlain Lessing Langbein Gilm Gryphius
Brentano Lafontaine
Strachwitz Claudius Schiller Schilling Kralik Iffland Sokrates
Katharina II. von Rußland Bellamy
Gerstäcker Raabe Gibbon Tschechow
Löns Hesse Hoffmann Gogol Wilde Vulpius
Luther Heym Hofmannsthal Gleim
Roth Klee Hölty Morgenstern Goedicke
Heyse Klopstock Kleist
Luxemburg Puschkin Homer Mörike
Machiavelli La Roche Horaz Musil
Navarra Aurel Musset Kierkegaard Kraft Kraus
Lamprecht Kind Moltke
Nestroy Marie de France Kirchhoff Hugo
Laotse Ipsen Liebknecht
Nietzsche Nansen Ringelnatz
Marx Lassalle Gorki Klett
von Ossietzky Leibniz
May Irving
vom Stein Lawrence
Petalozzi Knigge
Platon Kafka
Pückler Michelangelo Kock
Sachs Poe Liebermann Korolenko
de Sade Praetorius Mistral Zetkin

The publishing house tredition has created the series **TREDITION CLASSICS**. It contains classical literature works from over two thousand years. Most of these titles have been out of print and off the bookstore shelves for decades.

The book series is intended to preserve the cultural legacy and to promote the timeless works of classical literature. As a reader of a **TREDITION CLASSICS** book, the reader supports the mission to save many of the amazing works of world literature from oblivion.

The symbol of **TREDITION CLASSICS** is Johannes Gutenberg (1400 – 1468), the inventor of movable type printing.

With the series, tredition intends to make thousands of international literature classics available in printed format again – worldwide.

All books are available at book retailers worldwide in paperback and in hardcover. For more information please visit: www.tredition.com

tredition was established in 2006 by Sandra Latusseck and Soenke Schulz. Based in Hamburg, Germany, tredition offers publishing solutions to authors and publishing houses, combined with worldwide distribution of printed and digital book content. tredition is uniquely positioned to enable authors and publishing houses to create books on their own terms and without conventional manufacturing risks.

For more information please visit: www.tredition.com

The Log of a Noncombatant

Horace Green

Imprint

This book is part of the TREDITION CLASSICS series.

Author: Horace Green
Cover design: toepferschumann, Berlin (Germany)

Publisher: tredition GmbH, Hamburg (Germany)
ISBN: 978-3-8495-0581-3

www.tredition.com
www.tredition.de

Copyright:
The content of this book is sourced from the public domain.

The intention of the TREDITION CLASSICS series is to make world literature in the public domain available in printed format. Literary enthusiasts and organizations worldwide have scanned and digitally edited the original texts. tredition has subsequently formatted and redesigned the content into a modern reading layout. Therefore, we cannot guarantee the exact reproduction of the original format of a particular historic edition. Please also note that no modifications have been made to the spelling, therefore it may differ from the orthography used today.

Preface

In the following pages the ego is thickly spread. Their publication is the result of persuasion from many sources that, before returning to the war zone, I should put into connected form my personal experiences as correspondent during the first year of the War of Nations. A few of these adventures were mentioned in news letters from the Continent, where I limited myself so far as possible to descriptions of armies at war and peoples in time of stress; but the greater part of them were merely jotted down from time to time for my own benefit in "The Log of a Noncombatant."

Contents

The Log Of A Noncombatant

Chapter I

From Broadway To Ghent

When the war broke out in August, 1914, I was at work in the City Room of the "New York Evening Post." One morning, during the first week of activities, the copy boy handed me a telegram which was signed "Luther, Boston," and contained the rather cryptic message: — "How about this fight?"

It was some moments before I could recall the time, more than two years before, when I had last seen the writer, Willard B. Luther, Boston lawyer, devotee of some, and critic of many kinds of sport.

We had been sitting on that previous occasion — a crowd of college fellows, including Luther and myself — in a certain room in Cambridge, Massachusetts, not far from the University in that neighborhood where Luther had attended the Law School and the rest of us, on our respective graduation days, had received valuable pieces of parchment with the presidential signature attached. The conversation had already run through the question of Votes for Women, progressive politics, and prize-fights, and before the card game began it had settled on the last-named, chiefly because of my own vainglorious description of adventures at Reno, Nevada, at the time of the Jeffries-Johnson battle for the heavyweight championship of the world. I remember telling with some gusto of my first newspaper interview — one with "Bob" Fitzsimmons, then the Old Man of the ring, and "Gentleman" Jim Corbett, who was Jeffries' trainer at Reno.

"I had always wanted to see that performance," said Luther, "and would have gone in a flash if I could have got any one to make the trip with me. But remember this fact: whenever the next big fight is held I'm going with you." Later in the evening we shook hands on the proposition.

At the time that Luther's telegram came I was planning to start for the Continent as Staff Correspondent of the "New York Evening Post" and Special Correspondent of the "Boston Journal." Remembering that Cambridge agreement I immediately wired:—

"Yes. This fight will do."

So that is how it came to pass that Luther and myself boarded the Campania together, landed in Liverpool, cast about for ways and means of getting into the scrimmage, and for the first month and a half of my four months of wandering on the Continent were brother conspirators, until the duties of partnership called my friend home and left me without a companion in adventure.

In London we absorbed to some extent a heavy British fog and to a greater extent British public opinion. We marveled at the exterior calm of a nation plunged in the greatest of wars, yet fighting, so it seemed at the time, with its top hat on and its smile still undisturbed. Across the English Channel three days later the Dutch steam packet Princess Juliana carried us safely through mine fields and between lanes of British torpedo boats and torpedo boat destroyers. We landed on the Continent at Flushing. Thence we headed for The Hague, Holland, the neutral gateway of northern Europe, where we found the American Minister, Dr. Henry van Dyke, and his first secretary, Marshall Langhorne, shouldering the work of the American Legation in its chameleonesque capacity as bank, post-office, detective bureau, bureau of information, charity organization, and one might even say temporary home for the stranded travelers of every rank and nation.

Antwerp, the temporary capital of Belgium, was at this time invested, but not yet besieged, by the German army. On the south the city was already cut off by several regiments of the Ninth and Tenth German Army Corps under General von Boehn. The River Scheldt and the Dutch border formed a wall on the north and west. It was to Antwerp, therefore, that we determined to go. After listening to the usual flood of warnings against entering the fighting zone, and drinking our fill of stories of atrocity and hate which every refugee brought across the border into Holland, we took a couple of reefs in our baggage, and, hoisting our knapsacks, set our course for the temporary Belgian capital. By rail we traveled south across the level fields and lush green meadows of Holland, over bridges ready to be dynamited in case of invasion, and through training camps of the 450,000 Dutch soldiers then mobilized along the border. At a little town called Eschen the train stopped because the Belgians had torn up the tracks.

Seated on the cross-piece of a joggling two-wheeled ox cart, moving at the rate of not more than four miles an hour, with a dumb specimen for a driver, and a volume of Baedeker for interpreter and guide, we got our first glimpse of the hideous thing called war. Judging from the looks of the country and the burning villages, we were on the heels of a devastating army. For three, four, and five miles on either side of the road beautiful trees lay flat upon the ground. It was not until we saw groups of Belgian soldiers tearing down their own walls and hedges and applying match and gasolene to those which still stood, that we realized that this was a case of self-inflicted destruction. Farmhouses, stores, churches, old Belgian mansions, and windmills were either in flames or smouldering ruins. Where burning had not been sufficient, powder and dynamite had been applied to destroy landmarks which for centuries had been the country's pride. As far as the eye could reach the countryside was flattened to a desert. It reminded me of the Salem fire, through which, while the piles of debris were still smoking, I had been taken in the "Boston Journal's" car. But instead of a single town, here for twenty miles along lay stretched a smouldering waste. The devastation was for the defensive purpose of giving an unobstructed view to the cannon of Antwerp's outer fortifications, which on that side covered one sector of the circle swept by her enormous guns. I should hesitate to mention the millions of dollars of self-inflicted damage to Antwerp's suburbs alone. Luther and I did not at the time have the military password. So that first day was a specimen in the matter of hold-ups and arrests. From the time that we started across the level plains which approach the city until we got through the double sector of forts, we were stopped, questioned, and searched by thirteen different groups of soldiers. There were marry occasions where, after one pair of stupid sentries had put us through the grill, a second pair, watching from a distance of thirty yards or so, promptly repeated the entire performance. As these fellows spoke only Flemish dialect, our conversations were not particularly fluent. Frequently there gathered around us a crowd of gaping peasants, and when the word "Americaine" came out, there were "Oh's" and "Ah" of astonishment, or as often, when our explanations were not believed, sibilant hisses that shaped themselves into the menacing word "Spion." We had been led to believe that sooner or later a wool-witted sentry would shoot first and investigate later; but so far they had simply crossed bayonets, or with their hands up and palms outward had signaled us to halt.

Our experience that day, as later events proved, was not an extraordinary occurrence for war-time, especially for those endeavoring to gain entrance to an invested city. But as our first and maiden adventure it somewhat shook our nerve. When the grilling was over we felt about as guilty as any criminal who has been put through the third degree as practiced in the old police department days, and I had several times to look over my passport and letters of credentials to persuade myself that I was really not a spy. Eventually we were permitted to pass the gates of the Gare du Nord. Once inside the city gates, we made our way into the Place Verte and went directly to the Hotel St. Antoine, whose proprietor sent our names to police headquarters. The St. Antoine was at that time the residence of the diplomatic corps and the Belgian ministers of state, and was fifty yards from the Royal Palace and across the street from headquarters of the Belgian General Staff.

There is no need of describing in detail Antwerp at the time of my first visit. One or two pictures will suffice to give a rough idea of its existence up to the time of the bombardment. Try to imagine, for example, going about your business in New York or Boston or Los Angeles (of course Antwerp is smaller than these) when your country, a territory perhaps the size of the New England States, was already two thirds overrun, burnt, smashed, and conquered by a hostile nation, whose forces were now within nineteen miles of the gates of the capital. Imagine that nation's warriors in the act of crushing your tiny army, whose remnants were already exhausted and on the verge of despair. Then picture a quaint, sleepy city, with shadowy alleys and twisting, gabled streets, in which every other store and house was decorated with King Albert's picture or draped in the red, black, and yellow banner of the country-a city whose atmosphere was charged with fear and suspicion and excitement. Sometimes a crowd of a thousand or two drew one toward the Central Station where bedraggled refugee families, just arrived from Liege, Termonde, Aerschot, and Malines, stood on street corner or wagon top and thrilled the crowd with tales of atrocities and the story of their flight from their burning homes to the south. Now and then the crowd parted before the clanging bell of a Red Cross ambulance rushing its load of bleeding bodies to the hospitals along the Place de Meir. Nurses, male or female, clung to the ambulance steps. The first one I saw made a vivid impression on me. She was an English-looking girl in a new khaki skirt, supporting with one hand what was left of a blood-dripping head,—the eyes and nose were shot away,—while out of the other hand she ate with apparent relish a thick rye-bread sandwich. Occasionally she waved remnants of the sandwich at the gaping crowd. It struck me as a peculiarly unnecessary exhibition of her callous fitness for the job of nurse.

During the daytime the ordinary things of life went on, for the good burghers and shopkeepers went about their business as usual, and, generally speaking, fought against fear as bravely as the soldiers in the trenches stood up against the German howitzers. It was only after dark (when martial law permitted no lights of any kind) that the city seemed to shiver and suck in its breath; doors were barricaded, iron shutters came down, and behind them the people talked in whispers. Military autos, fresh from the firing line, groaned and sputtered at the doorstep of the St. Antoine; soldiers with pocket lanterns stamped about the streets. From sheer nervousness after a day of confinement some citizens, in spite of warnings, groped about the more important avenues at night. Picture yourself on Broadway or Tremont Street, with not a light on the street gleaming from a window, and walking up and down with one hand on your wallet and the other in the pocket where your Colt automatic ought to be.

Such, very briefly, was the condition of Antwerp at the time when we arrived. That very evening word came in that the Belgian forces, which had been engaged with the enemy for five consecutive days of severe fighting, had retired behind the southern ramparts of the city.

During the night the stream of incoming wounded confirmed the news of battle. In the moonlight, and later in the gray dawn, I watched the long lines of Belgian hounds, pulling their rapid-fire guns out toward the trenches. Many times later I was destined to see them. They made a picturesque and stimulating sight—those faithful dogs of war —fettered and harnessed, their tongues hanging out as they lay patiently beneath the gun trucks awaiting the order to go into action, or, when the word had been given, trotted along the dusty roads, each pair tugging to the battle front a lean, gray engine of destruction.

For our purpose the best approach to Brussels was by way of Ghent. Luther pushed on ahead while I was finishing a story. The following morning, shouldering my knapsack, which now contained an extra supply of army rations, and carefully stuffing my different sets of credentials in different pockets (one for Belgian, one for German, and one for English consumption), I crossed the River Scheldt and made a slow and tortuous railway journey to Ghent.

Ghent lies thirty miles west of Antwerp. The trip took seven hours. During the course of it I passed north of the Belgian lines and through the western sector of forts, that is to say, Fort St. Nicholas, Fort Haesdonck, and Fort Tete de Flandre. It was the same road along which Winston Churchill's English marines and the remnant of the Belgian forces retreated after the fall of Antwerp.

Ghent resounded with praises of its American Vice-Consul, Julius Van Hee, a hair-trigger politician and a live wire if there ever was one. Van Hee, with his intimate knowledge of four languages and the Yankee knack of being on the right spot at the right time, twice saved blood-shed in the streets of Ghent and in one instance probably prevented a repetition of the scenes at Louvain.

In Ghent I again found Luther, with a fine young rumor in his pocket —a rumor which turned out to be correct—that six German spies were to be executed next morning at sunrise. The place mentioned was behind the museum in a public park.

"I suppose we'll take it in," said Luther.

"I don't know about that," I answered; adding that, although executions might be part of the day's work for a war correspondent, I drew the line at seeing my first murder before breakfast. The tip was correct enough except that it mentioned the wrong park.

The following noon the Military Governor, according to regulations, caused to be posted circulars announcing that the men had been put to death; but at all events I am glad to say that at that early date I did not have the experience of watching six blindfolded wretches backed up against a wall, of seeing the officer drop his arm as a signal, and of hearing the fatal crack of a dozen muskets, as the bodies collapsed like a telescope, crumpled inward with the chin upon the chest, and fell forward to the earth.

Chapter II

The Second Bombardment Of Termonde

September 15th was our day with Henry Verhagen, the tall gray alderman of the town that was once Termonde.

During all the time I was with him Verhagen did not speak a bitter word. On the contrary, he was calm—particularly calm as he stood beside the mound where the Belgian soldiers were buried in the center of the ruined town, pointed to the pile of bricks where he had lived, and told us how in two nights he had lost 340,000 francs, his son, his factory, and his home. It was from him, from the burgomaster's wife, and from a priest that we learned the story of the city that had ceased to be.

It was the night before that I had wandered into Ghent alone, without even the excitement of getting arrested. Luther, who became restive early the next morning while I was jotting notes in the log-book, went off in search of adventure. Because of the influence exerted by Vice- Consul Van Hee an arrangement was very soon made whereby a Belgian Government car and chauffeur were placed at our disposal. We had no laissez-passer for the firing line; but we were accompanied by the United States Consul and not governed by any stipulation as to our destination. In our Belgian car, decorated with all the American flags we could find, and "American Consular Service" pasted in huge letters on the windshield and side flaps, we raced along the Boulevard de l'Industrie, swung into the southern suburbs, and, once outside the city limits, we opened up the exhaust and threw down the throttle as Van Hee shouted out the order: — "To Termonde!"

Termonde was at that time the scene of determined fighting between units of the ninth German Corps and the Belgian defenders. Situated as it is, twenty-one miles southeast of Ghent, it marks the southwest corner of a square formed by Louvain and Termonde on the south, by Ghent and Antwerp on the north. It controlled the bridge over the River Scheldt and with it an important approach to Antwerp, the capital at that time of Belgium. The heavy German siege guns, capable of demolishing a first-class fort at a range of several miles, could not have crossed the river so easily at any other point. For this reason the Germans particularly wanted Termonde—an open bridge to Antwerp was always worth the taking. The town had already at that time been captured and recaptured; wounded and refugees were swarming into Ghent full of battle stories and tales of terrible atrocities. So it was Termonde that we vowed we would see.

We first saw Verhagen trudging in the same direction as ourselves on the level, dusty road two miles southwest of Ghent. As we approached a cross-road marked by a tavern, a couple of direction-posts, and nondescript stucco buildings, we made out two Belgian sentries, with their rifles lifted overhead and indulging in some acrobatic exercises which we interpreted as a signal to halt. Van Hee swapped cigarettes with them and gossiped in their native tongue, in return for which they gave us some good advice. They warned us to pay no attention to sign-posts, which, in order to fool the enemy, were either marked with false names or else were pointed in the wrong direction. While we were talking, a tall gray alderman came along the road with a greasy package under his arm and at his side a priest—one of those ubiquitous black-robed figures with a hat like an inverted oatmeal bowl.

"Where to?" asked the Vice-Consul of Ghent.

"A Dendermonde," (to Termonde), answered Verhagen, sizing us up as strangers, and using French instead of the local Flemish dialect.

"You know the road?"

"Yes, well," said Verhagen; and so, partly because of charity and partly because we could have him as a useful guide, we took him into the car.

As we sped through the level lanes of poplars, challenged as usual by every Belgian regular or Garde Civique who could boast a uniform, the smooth green meadows of Flanders with their trim hamlets of stucco and tile seemed to deny the reports of savagery we had heard the night before. We had been told, and we had read, of German atrocities, and we had talked with survivors of Louvain. There was pillage, burning, and looting in Louvain, we had agreed, but the cruelty to women and children was the better part myth. And at all events, there was a semblance of cause for that. Perhaps there had been more resistance, more sniping by citizens than generally known, and perhaps the German side had not been fully explained.

Then suddenly Termonde lay before us. The center of the bridge was gone. Splintered timber sticking on end lay in the mud at the river's side, along with iron beams torn by the charges of dynamite. The current was choked with masses of steel and wood. We crawled across some temporary beams reconstructed by Belgian engineers, and entered the ruins with a handful of Termonde's citizens who had come back for the first time to see what was left of their homes.

"I will take you to the center," said Verhagen. "That is where my house was."

A quarter of a mile behind us, as the alderman sat upon a rock beside the gravestone, lay the thin neck of the Upper Scheldt, less than one hundred yards wide at this point, where it curved between the lines of charred and flattened buildings. We could still see the rush of water tumbling and splashing through the wreckage of the bridge we had just crossed. Twice it had been dynamited and twice rebuilt in part, so that at present a single line of slippery beams, suspended a few feet above the water and supported by some heavy wire, was all that remained between ourselves and the retreating road to Ghent. From the direction of Alost came the desultory boom of German guns; across the stream behind us the Belgian outposts whiled away the time with cigarettes and cards. Shaggy horses dozed against the gun trucks, and the men of artillery, some stretched at full length in the sun, others sitting bolt upright with arms folded, slept soundly on the gun carriages. We could hear the stream gurgling. We could hear the creak of a lazy windmill, and, coming somewhere from the smoking piles, the hideous howl of starving hounds. Of other human sounds there were none except the voice of Verhagen.

Ten days before Termonde had been a thriving town; that day it was a heap of smouldering ashes. America had heard a good deal about Tirlemont and Louvain, but not much of Termonde. Because this was a war of millions, it did not count in the news—for it was only a community of twelve thousand inhabitants, as pretty and quaint as the province of Flanders boasts, the prosperous center of its rope and cordage manufacture, with fifteen hundred houses, barracks, two statues, a town-hall, five churches, an orphan asylum, and a convent.

Now only one of the churches stood, as well as the building where the officers were quartered, the Museum of Antiquity, and perhaps a dozen others. Across the moat, which led to the gateway of what were formerly the inner fortifications, were piles of rotting horseflesh. The bronze statue of De Smet, the Jesuit missionary, looked calmly on the scene. All the rest was blotted out. There was no sign of hot-tempered impetuous work of a handful of drunken Uhlans, a fire started in anger and driven by the wind throughout the entire town. There was not a breath of wind. That the night was calm was shown by the fact that here and there single houses, even houses built of boards, were spared at the commander's word. The convent was burnt and pillaged, stones and mortar littered the street in front of the Hotel de Ville, and upon the sidewalk lay the famous bells which came crashing to the street below when shells burst in the belfry. From cellar to garret nearly every remaining house was systematically drenched with naphtha and the torch applied, and when all was over hundreds of gallons were tossed into the River Scheldt. Over a small group of houses in the poorer section of the city, where the prostitutes were quartered, grim Prussian humor, or perhaps a sense of value received, had prompted the conquerors to write in great white chalk marks in German script, "Gute Leute. Nicht brennen!" (Good people. Do not burn!)

For an hour we walked through the silence of ashes and stone, stumbling over timber and debris, tangled and twisted wire, a fallen statue, broken bells or the cross-piece of a spire; we made our way through piles of beds, chairs, singed mattresses, and stepped over the carcass of a horse with its belly bloated and flies feasting on its glassy eyes. We entered an apothecary shop where the clock still ticked upon the counter. Thinking there could be no reason of war to call for the destruction of the orphan asylum, we entered its portals to investigate. Before us lay burnt beds and littered glass. We searched what ten days before had been a convent, and crawled over heaps of logs and brick into narrow alleys that reminded one of Naples or Pompeii—alleys where the walls stood so close as to hide the light of sun but not the odor of charred vats and sewage and smouldering, smelling things, long dead. Not far from there the way widened into the light, and before us, breaking the rays of sunset, stood the cross above a heap of cobblestones.

"They are buried here," said Verhagen, "and here too is my house."

Another alderman, a friend of Verhagen, who had been allowed to remain in Termonde most of the four days that the Germans stayed, had the story detailed in his little pocket diary. On Thursday, September 3, he said, he was just leaving his rope and twine factory when he heard the sounds of musketry to the south. A small force of Belgian outposts were completely surprised by a part of the Ninth German Army Corps under General von Boehn. They were completely outclassed. Before retreating, however, they let the enemy have a couple of volleys. In the return fire they lost six of their men. They then retreated into the town and across the bridge.

Nothing happened after dark, but the next morning at nine o'clock the cannonading started. Inside of half an hour, according to the villagers, the entire German force of the One Hundred and Sixty-second and One Hundred and Sixty-third Uhlans and the Ninetieth Regiment of infantry of the Ninth Army Corps were in the town. They entered simultaneously by three different roads. The burgomaster was ordered immediately to provide rations for the regiment. But the burgomaster was away. He was given twelve hours to return. When he did not return, the burning began, according to the townspeople.

"The soldiers did not wish to burn the town," said one man; "but the orders were orders of war." He recounted that four Uhlans entered his house with a bow, and a knock at the door, politely helped themselves to his cellar, drank a toast to his wife, put his chairs in the street, and sat there playing his phonograph. They said they were sorry, but the house must be burnt. But before pouring on the naphtha and lighting the flame they freed his canary bird. Verhagen and the priest agreed that fright brought on an attack to a woman about to become a mother, and that she fell in the Rue de l'Eglise. A German lieutenant saw the trouble, put her on a stretcher made of window shutters, and called the German army doctor. She was sent to a field hospital and tenderly cared for until she and the child could be moved. Such incidents in strange relief, told by men who had lost everything, lent corroboration, if such were necessary, to the burden of their story of the relentless destruction of the town itself.

Our little band was the first to enter the ruins of Termonde after its abandonment by the Ninth German Army Corps. And by a coincidence, we were the last to leave. That very evening, at precisely the time we were crawling across the broken timbers that spanned the Scheldt and connected us with Belgium-owned Belgium, the Germans again pumped heavy artillery fire into the town. This was later known as the second German bombardment and occupation of Termonde. Because of superior artillery range, the attack had the cruel advantage of the man who can strike and still stay out of reach. On that evening at six-thirty, the Teutons sent a few warning shells into the debris, and then the first column of scouts entered simultaneously by the two southern gates. It was just at six-thirty that our party started back for Ghent.

As we crawled across on all fours the remaining beams cracked beneath our feet and the Belgian engineers called on us to hurry. "Oh, Tiber! Father Tiber," we thought as the last of us got across; but unlike Horatius at the bridge, we were on the right side when engineers applied the match to a small charge of dynamite, and the beams crashed and the remaining planks of Termonde's bridge writhed and twisted in the rushing waters.

Twenty-seven miles away, when we whirled through the gates of Ghent later in the evening, we said "Au revoir" to Verhagen and the mendicant priest, and went to our rooms. At midnight came a rap at the door; my gray-haired alderman broke into the room, bursting with the latest news, his eyes aflame with excitement.

"Revanche!" he exclaimed dramatically; "our enemies have paid for it in blood!"

Sure enough, after a few preliminary shells—a sort of here-we-come salvo—the head of the German column had entered, and a party of staff officers, for purposes of reconnaissance, immediately mounted the spire of the only remaining church. The officers of the Ninth German Army Corps swept the landscape with their glasses, but the level plains gave nothing to their sight. They saw only the ashes of Termonde, the river, and the straight stretch of sandy roads and stucco hamlets beyond.

They did not notice a valley of covered ground and a quarter-mile stretch of trees and shrubbery, where three squads of Belgian field artillery were neatly hidden. Here the men took cover at the first sound of cannonade. Quietly in their retreat the Belgian artillery officers had figured the range and elevation of the cathedral tower, not over fifteen hundred yards away. Just as darkness was setting in and the figures in the belfry were clearly visible, the battery sergeant sharply dropped his arm.

"C-r-r-m-p-h!" coughed the field pieces as the gunners drew the levers home. There were four sharp reports, four flashes of flame and smoke, the crescendo moan of tons of flying steel—and the church tower, the bells, and the German officers came crashing to the ground

Chapter III

Captive

Up to the day that Luther and I went through the Belgian trenches near Alost and got into the hands of the German outposts north of Brussels, we had not seen nearly as much fighting as we wished. We had looked upon the ear-marks and horrible results of battles; had heard guns, smelt the blood and ether of wounded, and seen the ruins over which had rolled the wave of battle. We knew that ahead of us there had been much fighting in the Sempst-Alost-Vilvorde- Tirlemont region. The Germans at that moment, if not actually advancing toward Antwerp, were skirmishing and making feints in every direction, with the ultimate disposition of their forces carefully concealed. Of course, we had no official permission to be at the front with either army; in fact, up to that point we had received nothing but official threats on the subject of what would happen to us in case we went ahead. But as no one did more than threaten, we kept on going, since we preferred that mode of procedure to sitting around in Paris or Berlin on the chance of one of those "personally conducted" tours of inspection, whose purpose is to show the correspondent everything except actual fighting. It was our hope during that early part of the war to see as much as possible of the German army, realizing that, if captured, we should undoubtedly be sent either backward or forward along the German line of communication in conquered Belgium. Once within the German outposts we pleaded like Brer Rabbit not to be thrown into the German brier patch. So of course we landed in it. After a few days in Brussels they shipped us Eastward to Aix-la-Chapelle by way of Lou-vain, Tirlemont, and Liege.

It was two days after the second bombardment of Termonde—at 7 A.M., to be exact—that Luther and I started from Ghent for Brussels in a military automobile, the property of the Belgian Government, and again loaned for the occasion to Julius Van Hee, American Vice- Consul, then Acting Consul at Ghent. We carried with us a United States Government mail pouch, a packet of mail from Dr. Henry van Dyke, at The Hague, addressed to Brand Whitlock, the American Minister at Brussels, and another packet of mail from Henry W. Diederick, United States Consul-General at Antwerp. Mr. Van Hee hoped to obtain from the German authorities in Brussels some smallpox vaccine to take back to Ghent, where a smallpox epidemic was feared.

Once out of the town limits of Ghent we bowled along at top speed, with the American colors trembling fore and aft and impressive- looking signs pasted on windshield and side-flaps. The autumn rains descended heavily upon us, drenching everything except the carefully protected mail bags.

Six miles southeast of Ghent, we ran into a regiment of Belgian infantry moving back from the direction of Brussels, and farther on a squad of cavalry and some more cavalry outposts; then two companies of bicycle patrol, the men with their heads bent over the handlebars, Mausers slung over their shoulders, pedaling heavily through the mud and slush of a cold September storm. A few mitrailleuses, known as the Minerva type, and mounted on armored motor-cars, were trained on the ravine through which the road dipped a thousand yards ahead of us. They had sighted the German outposts on the crest of a hill opposite us about three quarters of a mile away. In a very poor kind of trench, hastily constructed in the beet-fields, and little more than body deep, the men lay on their bellies in the mud, nervously fingering their muskets and adjusting the sights. A third company of bicycle scouts were ordered to advance for the purpose of drawing fire.

I doubt if that particular body of men had ever before been under fire. Never was the fear of death more plainly written on human face. All of the men went ahead without flinching or failing, but the muscles of their jaws were knotted, their faces were the color of chalk, and one or two dismounted for a moment, subject to the physical effects of fear. I have seen men tremble before important physical contests: Jeffries, stepping into the prize ring at Reno, Nevada, ready for the beating of his life and the loss of reputation. I have seen murderers condemned to death. Charles Becker, as I watched him taking his death sentence that evening in the Criminal Courts Building, did not give one the same uncanny feeling as this handful of Belgian scouts pedaling out to meet the German fire. I do not intend to say the Belgians were not brave men, for this was an isolated instance. And indeed there was something gruesome about that little company offered for the slaughter, simply for the purpose of locating the German batteries. The men understood the meaning of the order and appreciated the odds against them.

The mitrailleuses pointed down the road we were headed on, and the Belgian gun-captain told us they were going to clean things up as soon as their own scouts drew fire and the first Teuton helmet appeared above the crest. Naturally we were ordered back. Had we continued on this road we should have been between the Belgian fire behind and the German fire in front, for the Germans would undoubtedly have mistaken us for a scouting party in an armored car. As it was, Luther jumped to the wheel and insisted on seeing the thing through. We went ahead for about half a mile. I told him that if the shrapnel began to burst too close he would find me tucked safely underneath the car examining the gasoline tanks or in the nearest farmhouse cellar, and I believe he would have. But nothing came close to us on that occasion. My real "baptism" was reserved for another day, because Van Hee suddenly wrenched the wheel from Luther and turned our machine down a side road. It was a case of out of the firing line into the frying-pan, for the side road led us into a trap from which there was no turning back.—the territory patrolled by the burly pickets of the Ninth German Army Corps, forming part of the Kaiser's army of occupation in Brussels.

Out of earshot, and certainly out of sight of that skirmish, we were speeding at a great rate along a level, lonely road flanked by beet-fields and long lines of graceful elms that shook hands overhead, when:

"HALT! WOHIN? WO GEHEN SIE?" rang suddenly out of the darkness as two figures jumped from behind a farmhouse and leveled their rifles at us. I shall always remember that sharp command as the cold, gray muzzles followed us like a sportsman covering a bevy of quail. Our fat Belgian chauffeur, violinist in times of peace, and posing that day as an American,—one of those men who look as if they would bleed water if you pricked them with a bayonet,—needed no second warning. Running the German gauntlet was not precisely his hobby. Down went the emergency brake and the car jolted to a sudden halt.

A bristle-whiskered German giant under a canvas-covered helmet stuck his head through the flaps, and for more than ten minutes he and another sentinel searched our knapsacks and credentials and inspected the Government mail pouches which we carried. The sentries were far from satisfied. We said little at first, realizing, nevertheless, that we had run between the opposing trenches and up to the German outposts without actually drawing fire. That, at least, was something of a comfort.

Then, as if the answer was the price of admission, the big one asked us if we had seen many British soldiers around Antwerp and Ghent. We had previously decided that the answer to such talk was, "None of your business." But the fellow's bayonet was infernally bright and sharp and his countenance like ice. It wasn't only the equinoctial rain that made us shiver.

While I was trying to limber up my German vocabulary he passed us along to his Ober-leutenant in the hut along the roadside. The Ober- Ieutenant was grave. He said we must report to army headquarters in Brussels, and that under no circumstances should we be allowed to return within the Belgian lines. In this way began our eight days' confinement within the lines of the German Army of the North under General von Boehn.

Just as we had been warned repeatedly, so we discovered in reality that to cross between two opposing lines was no joking matter. Bad enough, particularly in the early days of the war, to a correspondent without permission at the front. To work up from the rear (if you had permission) was at least according to the rules of the game. But to cross between hostile armies—that was the one forbidden act. The fact that we were with an American Consul was not sufficient. Three days later Van Hee was allowed to return, but the remainder of the party, that is to say, Willard Luther and myself, were given a free trip into German territory and incidentally more than a week's chance to study the German army from within.

Those next eight days Luther and I spent as willing and, on the whole, decently treated captives within the lines of the German Army of the North, talking freely with cultivated officers and grimy men of the ranks, and in this way learning much of the German war machine, the opinions of the officers and the men at their command. It would be interesting to tell how in Brussels we dodged from War Office to cafe, from cafe to consulate, from consulate back to War Office, and later were worried and watched and suspected; how we were shipped back across the German border on a combination Red Cross and ammunition train; how we were locked for much of the night in a half-mile tunnel of the northern Vosges Mountains, and there, in the groping darkness of our box-car prison, shared the soldier's biscuit and his bottle, so coming to know the Kaiser's private as a companion and not as the barbarian his enemies paint him.

The day after we got inside the German lines we went before Major Heinrich Bayer, at that time military commandant in Brussels in the absence of General von der Goltz. Jostling through the street and jamming the courtyard of the War Office was a crowd of a thousand persons—mothers, children, whole families begging for relief or permission to leave the city limits; German subjects trying to get passes, officials and employees of the civil administration taking orders from the military authorities. A relay of aides, orderlies, and secretaries led us from courtyard to corridor and from corridor to staff headquarters and into the Holy of Holies—the office of the commandant.

Grim, stern,—but courteous throughout the interview,—the major paced the floor beside his desk. He seemed anxious enough to be rid of the "crazy Americans" who had wandered through the Belgian and German lines, not altogether satisfied with their integrity, yet not wishing to take a hostile attitude. I asked him when he thought the war would be over. At the moment the German major, Vice-Consul Van Hee, and I were the only persons in the room.

"I do not know," he said, as if thinking aloud; "I really do not know. America is the only country that has not fired on us yet, but all the rest —" Then he added thoughtfully, "Perhaps it is better that you go. But you cannot return to Ghent or Antwerp; you must go back to Germany." He stopped as if he had gone too far, and then sharply commanded the orderly to remove us. Forty-eight hours later Mr. Van Hee got his release. To Luther and myself was given a curious sort of pass, beset with limitations, which at times caused us royal treatment and as often proved a fatal baggage tag. I have always believed a joker lay hidden somewhere in that document. It started with a flattering description of our status (as given by ourselves), but below it directed us to be taken into Aix-la-Chapelle, Germany, and under no circumstances to be returned within the Belgian lines. We had seen a great deal too much for that. In spite of our protestations of good faith and promises to keep dark what we had seen, the military authorities considered us much safer under German guard. We were to be taken on the southern route by way of Namur. To drive home the importance of obeying this order we were reminded of the regulation, printed in French and posted throughout the city, "that whosoever passed the city limits or approached the fighting line without military permit, or on the pretense of having such a permit, or whosoever deviated from the route laid down would be shot 'sur le champ.'" That same evening, however, army orders declared that the Namur route was closed. We got a second War Office pass sending us to Aix by way of Louvain, Tirlemont, and Liege. Armed with these we went down to an old Major Bock von W — — —, in charge of transportation at Schaerbeek, on the outskirts of the city.

I showed him the passes and said with a painful attempt at levity, "Major, we can't obey both of these, so we 're going to get shot either way we go. If it is all the same to you I would rather die on your route." To my great relief the old fellow laid back his gray head and emitted a series of long, loud Teuton laughs. He was the first German I had heard laugh and it did me good. I knew we were safe. On the understanding that the business was strictly confidential and that no other citizens or suspects were to know of it, he gave us a permit for the military trains. It had been the intention of the War Office to pack us under guard with the herds on one of those Government refugee trains. But to live and sleep with the soldiers as we were now to do, to see their marches, to absorb their uninformed and boastful talk, to study their guns, munitions, and equipment, was better than our highest hopes.

"You have to do a lot of quick transporting?" I asked before saying good-bye to Major von W— — —.

"Yes," was the answer. "They 're at us from all sides. Some of the men we are now transporting have been under fire in two countries, and now they will see service in a third." He knew that I had come from Ghent and from Antwerp, which the Germans were about to bombard, yet, to his credit, it should be said that he did not ask for information of Belgian activities. Similarly, although the soldiers, as a rule, and one man high in the civil government of Brussels, asked what was going on in Antwerp, it was noticeable that German officers recognized the obligations of neutrality.

Of how we left Brussels and of the first part of the eastward trip, I am going to quote from the jottings in the log-book, which was written up at some length after we left Aix-la-Chapelle:—

"Early on the morning of the 22d, I went up to Consul Watts's office to get the mail pouch I had promised him to carry. Luther and I then boarded a trolley car going northwest past the Gare du Nord and on to Schaerbeek, a junction on the outskirts of Brussels. Although the Major Bayer passes, with von W— — —'s counter-signature, got us as far as Schaerbeek, we were challenged by the guards at the railroad station. The stations were watched with the most astounding precaution. Of course there was no such thing as a ticket; once inside the gate you could jump a troop train, ammunition car, or blow up the track if you felt like it. Wherefore they guarded the stations carefully.

"At the gates had a terrible pow-wow with an officious Bavarian who called himself the Officer-of-the-Day. I played all my best German cards, including Count von Bemstorffs letter. At the end of half an hour our pig-headed officer shipped us back to Brussels. We returned to von W— — —, then in Brussels, who vised our pass with a note to the effect that although we were civilians, exceptional circumstances demanded our hurried return to Aix by military train.

"When we eventually got into the Schaerbeek station we had two hours to wait. Walked up and down the tracks or sat on the platform, keeping an eye on everything that was going on. Luther says I spent most of my time trying not to look like an Englishman. Occasionally, when we spoke a word of English, some officer would shoot us a 42 cm. glance and demand our papers. We were undoubtedly marked figures, because in the first place no civilians were allowed along the railway line, especially foreigners.

"Watched several westbound loads go by until about two o'clock, when they made up a combination train consisting of Red Cross coaches and empty freight trucks going back to Aix for fresh loads of men and ammunition. Aix is the great distributing center for the line of communication into northern Belgium. Most of the open cars were empty, barring occasional gun carriages on the way home for repairs; in the closed freight cars lay a few wounded first line men, a half a dozen male nurses, and some privates on furlough. Speaking of nurses, I haven't—so far at least-seen a woman nurse nearer the scene of action than a base hospital, i.e., one of the big hospitals in Antwerp, Brussels, or Ghent. Luther and I, closely followed by the two guards that had trailed us from the time we had got inside the station, climbed into a freight car, apparently used as a box stall on the out trip, and bare except for a pile of damp straw in one corner. Interminable journey. Most of the time we stood on sidings waiting for the outbound traffic. Made fair time to Louvain,—i.e., an hour and a half,—and stayed there two hours, for which I was thankful, as it gave me a chance to look around. Interviewed soldiers, citizens, and a Jesuit priest, of which more later. One hour more to Tirlemont. Then seven hours to Liege, where we arrived at 2 A.M., were smothered for two hours in that tunnel, and took six and three quarters hours more from Liege to Verviers—a distance of less than fifteen miles! It was another five hours to Aix.

"Saw tremendous troop movements along Brussels-Louvain-Verviers line of communication. During the first day thirty-five troop and transport trains went past us, moving towards the western frontier, the larger part to strengthen the German attack on Antwerp, which we had not long left behind us, others to discharge their loads as near as possible to Lille, Tournai, and Mons. The average train was twenty cars long, making about seven hundred carloads, with two hundred or more in each car, giving a total of more than 140,000 fighting men. We stopped counting at the end of the first day.

"After we left Louvain I got out occasionally and stretched my legs along the tracks, but Luther, not being able to talk German, stuck pretty close to his diggings. Had a great time at a little town called Neerwinden, where we stayed about half an hour. A crowd of soldiers from our train joined a group cooking supper in the moonlight at one of the soup kitchens along the tracks. They fed me lukewarm stew and slabs of rye bread, then went on singing and arguing without paying much attention to me. One bald-headed, stocky private told the crowd the news that von Hindenburg had captured Warsaw. Later a crowd of big brutes, apparently pretty drunk, swaggered down and clapped me on the back with a 'Who are you, my friend?'

"'Amerikaner,' I explained, not thinking it necessary to mention the war correspondent part. They set up a cheer, clapped me on the back, and finally lifted me to their shoulders for a triumphal ride up and down the railroad ties, all the time yelling out 'Amerikaner! Hurrah! Amerikaner!'

"A few hundred years seemed the night we spent locked in that box-car prison. A five-days' equinoctial storm had given way to the coldest day of the autumn: our car, raw and dank as a dungeon, joggled along endlessly until afternoon gave way to evening and evening to chilly night. Hour after hour we looked out upon the rolling fields and burnt farmhouses along the path where General von Emmich's army had passed. As the moon crawled up over the rain-bathed foothills of the Ourthe Mountains, the temperature dropped far below the freezing point. For ages we lay awake braced against the cold. The soldier next me, who had been through the fight at Maubeuge, coughed throughout the night—a hollow, retch ing cough. "Tuberculosis," the Red Cross doctor told me, although the fellow had got through his army tests all right.

Between two and four in the morning we stuck in the middle of a tunnel of the northern Vosges Mountains, two hundred feet, perhaps, beneath the surface of the ground. The sliding door on the left side of our car was locked: on the other side jagged walls, dripping wet to the touch, jutted so close that a thin man couldn't have walked between them and the car. Everywhere pitch blackness, the blackness of the tomb. The consumptive soldier pulled a candle from his kit, balanced it in the straw, and over it warmed his hands. If that candle had toppled over in the straw we wouldn't have had a rat's chance in the fire. It was impossible to get out of our car or to communicate with another except by tapping. The fellows in the next car must have been considerably frightened, for after about an hour they began yelling and pounding at the walls. All you could hear was a roaring sound that caromed against the walls of the cavern. Smoke from the engine drifted back to choke us. It hit the consumptive worst. The poor fellow began blowing and coughing, then rolled feebly on his back and gasped. During the worst of the smoke one of the soldiers in the next car set up a rollicking song, and others followed his example. We could hear the clank of beer bottles as they finished, the echoes of the song reverberating loudly, then faintly, then louder again up and down the length of that interminable vault. A draught of air cleared the smoke away and it didn't bother us again. At four in the morning we steamed out of the tunnel into the open. A little after that I must have dozed off, for I woke with a start when the consumptive stumbled over me.

"There you are," he said, throwing a bundle beside me; "I thought you'd need it."

Noticing, when he lit his pipe at dawn, that we had no army blankets and were pretty nearly frozen, this "barbarian" had jumped out of the car in the Liege freight yards, had run a quarter of a mile to the nearest army kitchen depot, and had stolen for us a couple of heaping blankets' full of warm, dry straw.

It was impossible to believe that these men had committed the atrocities reported at Termonde and Roosbeek, at Malines and Louvain. At close range it was easy to see that the prevalent conception of the "barbarians" was the purest kind of rot—the picture created and fostered by the Allied press, of a vicious and besotted beast with natural brutality accentuated by alcoholic rage. With such men as individuals it seemed to us that neutral observers could have no quarrel. To the Kaiser's privates who have been fighting for a cause they do not thoroughly understand, was due, we thought, the greatest respect; to the officers, too, who understand what they are doing and are game in the face of odds; and most of all to the suffering German people. But to the German war machine, we reflected, was due a terrible punishment — the lesson it must learn not only for Germany's enlightenment, but for the sake of civilization and humanity.

Chapter IV

A Clog Dance On The Scheldt

When the German major at Aix-la-Cha-pelle stamped on our passports:— "Gesehen. Gut Zum Austritt Kommandant 2 Kompagnie, Landsturm Batl. Aachen," we were free, so we thought, to shake the dust of Germany from our feet. Hoisting our rucksacks, we gave up box cars in favor of a civilized passenger train, northward bound, and at noon crossed the Dutch border at Simplefeldt.

For three hours we talked English, consulted maps, took notes, and asked questions where and when we pleased. The holiday cost us dear. At the end of that time we were under lock and key in the town of Maastricht, the Province of Limburg, and the supposedly free and neutral Kingdom of the Netherlands. We suspected at the time, and in view of what I learned upon a later trip to Berlin I am quite certain, that the long arm of the German Secret Service had reached out for us across the border.

Having started from Antwerp during its investment, but prior to its siege by the German army, we were now on the third stage of a round trip which was to land one of us back in the Belgian temporary capital in time for the bombardment. During the previous two weeks we had been stopped, questioned, and sometimes examined, no less than one hundred and thirty times. Thirteen, we calculated, was our average number of hold-ups on our early "marching days"; that is to say, during those wanderings which led us by foot, train, ox cart, and automobile past the double sector of Antwerp's fortifications, through the Belgian fighting lines to Ghent and Termonde, and thence into the arms of the German pickets on the outskirts of Brussels.

And now, as the heavy door of the Maastricht police headquarters slammed in our faces, and the key rattled in the guardroom lock, my companion in crime threw down his hat and coat in rage. Between us we treated our fellow-prisoners to a quarter of an hour's tirade on the American citizen's right to freedom, swore that the Kingdom of the Netherlands would repent this outrage, and each of us politely assured the other it was all the other fellow's fault.

All of which, though true, had no effect on the sniffling young woman across the way, nor the sleeper on the hardwood bench next mine, nor the bald-headed, big-lipped police sergeant who bent over his desk in the corner, impervious to these usual outbursts of the newly arrested, as he laboriously scrawled in the police blotter the report of the day's round-up.

"Sit down!" he bellowed as I advanced toward the pen door, and tried to open it.

When he resumed his scratching I did my best to explain in a German-French-Dutch dialect of my own invention that we wished to see Mons. le Commissaire at once; that we had only come to inspect the concentration camp of German and Belgian prisoners, and that we were leaving town that day. I particularly emphasized this point. We were, in fact, I assured him in several different ways, leaving that very afternoon—as soon as the disagreeable mistake of our arrest was rectified. He may or may not have understood this: at all events, he wore an expression as blank and graven as Jack Rose upon the witness stand. His only answer was a vacant stare at the pit of my stomach, followed by a slow scratch-scratching on the police blotter.

In fact our arrest on that occasion was rather a Jack Rose affair; that is to say, it started by our being invited to headquarters, suspicious but not certain of our status until we finally landed behind the iron doors. Without doubt Maastricht authorities were waiting for us even as we stepped off the train, showing that we were doomed from the time we left the border. Our captor, an unctuous, pink-cheeked politzei, made his appearance not far from the internment camp. Where were we going, and why?

"To see the prisoners," we said.

"It is possible," said the spider to the fly, "zat I can get for you permission if you will come to ze guardhouse. Ze capitain is there."

The "guardhouse" proved a precinct police station, and the captain was not there: instead we found a mixed crowd of civilians and militaires who looked us over and shook their heads. Next we were taken to military headquarters \n the center of the town. For fifteen minutes we hunted the evasive captain while I ran through my head the various sets of credentials stuffed in different pockets; for, being in Dutch territory, although only a few miles from the Belgian frontier on one side and the German frontier on the other, I was not quite certain which to produce. Among my letters I carried one from the German Ambassador, Count von Bernstorff, to the Foreign Office in Berlin; one from Professor Hugo Munsterberg at Harvard, and a note from the secretary of the Belgian Legation at The Hague. Unfortunately I did not have with me at the time a very helpful letter from Colonel Roosevelt, ending with the statement that the bearer "is an American citizen, a non-combatant, and emphatically not a spy." I had promised the Colonel to use this, my trump card, only in case of necessity—and once, on a later occasion, I did so with immediate effect. On the whole, I now decided in favor of a United States passport decorated with my picture and enough vises to resemble the diplomatic history of the Continent.

"The captain is not here. We go to the commissaire at headquarters," said the polite politzei. It was then that we cut loose, told him to bring the commissaire or the burgomaster to us, and started to walk off. It was a bad move. So far he had handled us with a velvet grip, but at the first sign of insurrection he showed his teeth, locked arms with each of us, and, signaling another officer to follow, forthwith marched us off to police headquarters and our ultimate resting-place, the guardroom cell.

How long we stayed there I don't know—long enough, at all events, to get a glimpse of the Dutch police system and the third degree as practiced in the Lowlands. There swung open a great iron door leading to the street and the market-place, not so large but fully as busy as Washington Market the week before Thanksgiving. Through it, sobbing and screaming, their hats gone and their hair torn, came two women, roughly handled by gendarmes and followed by a mob escort. They were thrown weeping and expostulating into an adjoining cell. A gendarme came out with trickles of blood on his face. He mopped his brow and complained of feminine finger-nails. Close behind him followed a male friend of the imprisoned women. He pleaded with the sergeant at the desk, while the moans of the women, under pressure to confess their crime, came from their cell. But Jack Rose only scratched and scratched monotonously, and now and then gazed at the middle of the speaker's stomach.

In the mean time we fell back into our habit of talking for publication. With an intimacy that would have surprised those gentlemen we referred casually to Brand Whitlock, Dr. van Dyke, and the biggest Dutch and Belgian names we could think of. We suspected that Jack Rose and the man at our side understood more English than they pretended. At all events, it had its effect. In half an hour we were taken before the commissioner.

Two cigars lay on the edge of the table nearest us. I could see at a glance that we were free.

"Do you speak English?" I asked him.

"No," he answered in our native tongue; "only French, Flemish, German, and Italian—but not English." And with a grin he asked for our passports.

"You are for the American newspapers?"

"Yes," I answered—"one of us is a lawyer who writes occasionally. I am correspondent for a New York and a Boston paper, but I won't cable anything from here." For this reason, I explained, no movements of troops or news of military value could leak out.

"Ah, I see," said the commissioner who could not talk English. "An amateur correspondent and a slow correspondent. But correspondents are not at all tolerated in this province. It is five o'clock. You will board the train leaving this province at 5.16 P.M."

From Maastricht to the Dutch capital is, under usual conditions, a four-hour run to the north. During this trip we passed encampments and fortifications of the 400,000 well-drilled but poorly equipped troops which the Kingdom of the Netherlands, in the spirit of no negative neutrality, had mobilized along her borders. Whenever we crossed a bridge every window in the entire train was fastened down and there were strict orders against raising them. We discovered that under the boulders were carefully concealed large charges of dynamite ready for immediate use in case of invasion—so that Horatius need not be called upon while axe and crowbar were at work. The windows, it appears, were locked to prevent throwing out of lighted cigars or matches.

At one o'clock the next morning our train, delayed by war-time traffic, rolled into the Hague station, whence three days later, I was to start my lucky trip into Antwerp, the besieged.

Clog dancing and cognac helped to get me from The Hague back into Antwerp in time for its bombardment and capture by the German forces under General von Beseler. I happened to perform the clog dancing at a critical moment during a trip on a Scheldt River barge, thus diverting the attention of the river sentries from my lack of proper papers. While the pedal acrobatics were in progress my temporary friend, Mons. le Conducteur, reinforced the already genial pickets with many glasses of the warming fluid.

Willard Luther, my companion in and out of jail during the first part of the continental wanderings, was forced to leave for home the day after we got back to The Hague. He had five days to catch the Lusitania at Liverpool. Three of them he spent on a whirlwind trip trying to see action in northern Flanders, but, much to his disappointment, was called away before the final scrimmage at Antwerp. If he had succeeded in getting in, I rather fear the Massachusetts Bar would have lost a valuable member. He had an insatiable passion to be in the neighborhood of bullets and bombs— not, as I take it, that he really wanted to get hit—merely that he would like to see how close he could come.

On October 2d, strictest regulations were passed prohibiting entry within the fortifications of Antwerp without permit from the military governor, General de Guise. Three weeks earlier entry had been possible but difficult, and the feat was again easier after the German occupation. But during the city's days of trial the military lid was clamped and riveted. Except for those coming direct from England, the highest civil recommendations were valueless.

I had one of these,—a laissez-passer from Prince d'Eline, Secretary of the Belgian Legation at The Hague,—issued because of the fact that I was carrying a large packet of mail from the American

Legation at The Hague to Henry W. Diederick, United States Consul-General at Antwerp. I had also been entrusted with three hundred marks to be delivered to a German prisoner, Lieutenant Ulrici, known to have been wounded and captured in the fighting around Termonde, and believed to be lying in a hospital ship in the river or in Antwerp itself. The fact of carrying such money was of course against me as indicating German sympathy.

Because a large part of the railroad line between Eschen, Cappelen, and Antwerp had been torn up, because there would be many hold-ups, and because I couldn't speak a word of Flemish, I decided against the overland route. Hearing, however, that L. Braakman & Company, a grain and freight shipping concern, were running down barges from Rotterdam, I got a Belgian friend to call them up on my behalf. The result was a flat throw-down: without General de Guise's sanction I might not even cross the gangplank.

Nevertheless, I went to Rotterdam, crossed the river basin to the island from which the Braakman boats ran, and there saw a director of the company, who, fortunately, could speak both English and Flemish. He took me to the captain of the river barge, a low craft that looked a cross between a tugboat and a Hudson River scow. In less than three minutes my case was disposed of. Verdict: "C'est absolument defendu." It was time for a little "bluff." An hour later I returned with a new proposition, having in the mean time telegraphed Mr. Diederick either to meet me at the pier at Antwerp or to send a military permit. Displaying a copy of this telegram I suggested that I be allowed to board. If there was any one at Antwerp to meet and vouch for me, well and good; if not, they were at liberty to ship me back. That was my proposition.

"He may go as far as the border patrol, fifteen miles east of Antwerp," the captain said to my interpreter. "If the river sentries permit it he may then go as far as the Antwerp pier, but he cannot land."

We cast off Sunday, October 4th, at 6 A.M. The little Telegraaf III poked her nose through the blue-gray haze of a chilly October morning while the muddy waters of the Meuse slapped coldly against her bow. I stamped the deck a few times, wondering if there was an English-speaking soul aboard, and leaned up against the engine room until the odor of coffee and bacon lured me to the fo'castle hatch. A purple-faced giant, with thick lips that met like the halves of an English muffin blocked the companion-way.

"'Jour," growled the face as though it hated to say it, then pointed to the food and cognac. This was Monsieur le Conducteur, ship's cook, barkeeper, and collector of fares.

In the center of a dark cabin, littered with charts, pails, and Flemish newspapers, was a kitchen table. Now and then a smoking oil lamp flared up to throw a light on the faces of my fellow-passengers, five of them in addition to the captain and Mons. le Conducteur. They were, as I discovered later, Mons. A. Albrecht, a leading alderman of Antwerp and a friend of Mons. Vos, the burgomaster; a light-haired Belgian piano salesman who could speak five languages; Mile. Blanche Ravinet, of looks beautiful and occupation unknown; and two others. From the suddenness with which the conversation stopped, I judged they had been discussing "ze American." They were welcome to say what they liked barring the word "spion."

For hours we chugged steadily along, catching a fair tide on the lower Meuse, and sliding past the neat little towns of Dordrecht, Papendrecht, and Willemstad, through the Hollandische Diep and the Krammer Volkerak. After that the Telegraaf III worried through the canals and systems of locks which virtually cut the neck of Tholen from the mainland, and, when the last of these had been accomplished, splashed into the great basin of the East Scheldt A Dutch gunboat cut across our bows, signaling us to halt. An officer boarded us to study the freight invoices.

Farther upstream a launch came alongside, making fast fore and aft, while two Belgian river sentries, in long blue coats and faded drab trousers, poked their bearded heads above the rail. This, then, was what the captain meant by the border patrol.

Now, as luck would have it, the day was cold: we were the first boat to come through the locks for some hours, and apparently the river sentries had had no breakfast. So they dove into the fo'castle, where Mons. le Conducteur produced bread and cognac. I at once ordered Mons. le Conducteur to get a second round of liquid refreshment for our military guests. Conversation flowed. The soldiers drummed on the table to keep their hands warm and in a moment of inspiration I showed them how the darkies in our country warm their feet.

"Clog dance," I explained.

"Encore," shouted the piano salesman. "That is splendid."

"Pleaz again! Oh, pleaz!" echoed Mile. Blanche. "See, every one, ze grand American foot game."

The fat-faced conducteur, with whom I had suddenly grown in favor, repeated the cognac treatment on the sentries. Before I knew it, they had me alongside the table, one hand steadied against a thwart of the swaying cabin, my head in the smoke of the oil lamp, my feet pounding and kicking, as it seemed, at the very door of Antwerp. The piano salesman shouted rag-time, Mile. Blanche drummed time on the bench, and the river sentries pounded time with their rifle butts.

"Encore!" they shouted when I sat down with aching legs.

All at once the launch alongside gave an angry toot, for the officer wanted his men back: there were other boats to be examined. The sentries glanced quickly at our papers, not reading, I am sure, a word of mine, speedily cast off ropes, and disappeared guiltily and somewhat unsteadily over the larboard rail.

An hour later the Telegraaf III took the river's turn, swinging past Fort St. Philippe, until we could see the gray-blue spire of the Cathedral of Notre Dame with its intricate network of stone silhouetted against the autumn sunset. Mr. Diederick was not at the pier to meet me, nor was there a military passport from General de Guise.

"Stay by me," said Alderman Albrecht. As each of the pier sentries saluted him he said a whispered word, and apparently his word was good, for the American "foot game" artist was allowed to pass. Perhaps Alderman Albrecht had decided that German spies don't clog-dance.

Though not officially admitted to the besieged city, I went at once to my old stand, the Hotel St. Antoine, now converted into British Staff Headquarters. At sundown a mist crept up from the river, and through it we heard a roar of welcome and the rumble of heavy artillery. Charging down the Avenue de Keyser came a hundred London motor-busses, Piccadilly signs and all, some filled, some half-filled, with a wet-looking bunch of Tommies, followed by armored mitrailleuses, a few 6.7 naval guns, officers' machines, commissary and ammunition carriages—the first brigade of Winston Churchill's army of relief, which for five days was destined to make so valiant, but so short, a fight against the overwhelming German army.

Chapter V

The Bombardment Of Antwerp

There was something typically British in the way those Englishmen went about the defense of Antwerp. In the streets and barracks, and more especially at the Hotel St. Antoine, British Staff Headquarters, where I stayed until its doors were closed, I saw them at close range during that week of horror. Once when I was eating with a company of marines near their temporary barracks, they gave me the password to the trenches, and, although I only got out as far as the inner line of forts on that day, it gave me an opportunity to observe the work of the men under long-range firing. At the St. Antoine, ten or a dozen officers were quartered; others clanked in and out for hurried conferences in the corridors or disappeared into the smoking-room, whose heavy doors with the sign, "Reservee pour la Gouvernement Anglaise," hid Winston Churchill, then First Lord of the English Admiralty, and his portmanteau of war maps.

Here was Belgium's last stronghold on the verge of downfall: the outer line of forts had already fallen; Forts Wavre, St. Catherine, Waelham, and Lierre were already prey to the Krupp mortars; the German hosts were swarming across the River Nethe, six miles to the city's south, and the cowering populace in their flight made the streets terrible to look upon.

Yet at the St. Antoine there was no particular flurry—so far, at least, as the officers were concerned. At night they worked over their war maps; in the daytime they went out to the forts. They would get up in the morning, an hour or two earlier than the average business man, have a comfortable breakfast, smoke a cigar for half an hour or so, and talk things over. Then their military automobiles came trembling and sputtering to the doorsteps, and in groups of fours and fives they went out to the firing line. If only two or three of a group returned, you would naturally have to draw your own conclusions as to the fate of the rest.

Those English gentlemen went about their jobs of life and death with the same detached coolness as if their hunters were being saddled, or they were waiting for the referee's whistle in Rugby football. Their attitude was infernally exasperating; yet you couldn't help taking off your hat to their sublime nerve and indifference.

I overheard a typical remark when matters were in this critical state. It came from a handsome, curly-headed officer, noticeable not only for his apparent efficiency, but because he didn't let the game of war interfere with his attentions to the little Princess de Ligne. The latter was nursing her brother, who had been shot through the back of the neck during a raid through German lines. She was a princess in rank, and a queen in looks. Thirty hours before the first shell burst into the Place Verte—Monday morning, it was—this fellow rapped at my door. He had wandered into the wrong pew, for his words were obviously intended to hurry up a brother officer with whom he was to take the morning ride to the firing line. Sticking his curly, sunburnt head around the corner he drawled in inimitable British intonation:-

"I say, old chap, do hurry along; this is no ORDINARY occasion, you know."

In the Royal Belgian Palace there happened a few hours before the bombardment an incident revealing the simplicity and kindliness of King Albert's character. In connection with it, it is necessary to speak of Harold Fowler, a New Yorker and Columbia College graduate, who helped to save the public buildings of Antwerp, and later entered the Allied ranks as a fighter. When the war broke out, Fowler was private secretary to Ambassador Page in London. In November he got a commission in the Royal Horse Guards, known as the "Blues." While the Germans were pressing hard on Antwerp, the German commander, as I have mentioned elsewhere, asked that a diagram of the city of Antwerp, with plans and location of the cathedral, the Hotel de Ville, and the more important works be sent to him in order that he might find the range and avoid firing on them. Neutrals were to carry the plans through; and Fowler and

Hugh Gibson, secretary to the American Minister at Brussels (Brand Whitlock), volunteered.

Two days before the bombardment Gibson went to the Royal Palace at Antwerp where General de Guise and his staff were in conference. Fowler trailed along, but, not liking to enter, walked up and down the hallway, hands in his pockets, admiring the portraits half-hidden in the darkness of the foyer. A tall figure approached and in French asked who he was. Fowler replied that he was an American and was waiting for Gibson.

"I see," said the figure, then speaking in English, "that you are interested in pictures."

"Very much," answered Fowler.

"Then, would you like to see those in the Royal Chambers upstairs?"

Fowler hesitated, feeling like an intruder, but the figure insisted upon leading him upstairs. When they got into the light, Fowler turned to examine his kind friend. To his utter astonishment he saw that it was Albert, King of the Belgians!

By that time we of Antwerp were getting a very fair imitation of a city besieged. Water supply had already been cut off for some days. There was just enough for cooking purposes; bathing and such pleasantries were out of the question—even for Royalty. According to the French maid in my corridor, Winston Churchill managed to get a shave by ordering tea sent to his room and using the hot water for shaving lather.

Monday, October 5th, the night before the city emptied itself of non-combatants, was almost a festive occasion at the St. Antoine. The British entry gave tremendous confidence to the stricken city and the tired Belgian soldiers—a bit of pride before the fall. New faces turned up, friends in the English army met, shook hands, and discussed the outlook. One was even reminded of lighter occasions, such as the Copley-Plaza in Boston or the Hotel Taft in New Haven before an annual Harvard-Yale battle. At the head of a long table in the center of the dining-room sat the First Lord of the British Admiralty, looking rather thoughtful, his baldish head and Trinity House uniform standing out in contrast to the service uniforms of the younger men around him. At the same table were commissary officers, sergeants, aide-de-camps, Hugh Gibson, Harold Fowler, and somewhat farther down the Russian Minister and my curly-headed officer, chatting over his coffee with little Princess de Ligne.

In the flash of an eye these scenes changed to scenes of terror.

The news leaked out, and spread like wildfire, that the Kaiser's men had crossed the River Nethe and had placed their big guns within range of the city. It was not until forty-eight hours later that the populace saw a handful of Flemish posters pasted in out-of-the-way corners—posters signed by the Civil Government—which thanked the populace "for retaining until the present time their praiseworthy sangfroid, and regretting that the responsibilities of their office necessitated their own removal to a neighborhood more safe."

Queen Elizabeth, whom danger made a democrat, walked right into my hotel, if you please, and stopped casually to say good-bye to the Russian Minister. The crowd outside did not know she was leaving for Ostend under cover of darkness—they cheered her loudly just the same. She is a spunky sort of queen.

Then came the flight. You knew the fear of the Germans had got into their blood when waiters dropped their plates and dishes and ran; when shops, houses, hotels closed and the people melted away; when the French chambermaid besought with frightened eyes that Monsieur take her away to England, and when the hotel proprietor disappeared without even asking for his bill.

There were other sights that did one good to see: such as gray-haired Mrs. Richardson, venerable figure of a British nurse, with six wars to her credit and a breastful of decorations from four different governments, who refused to leave her hospital even if it was blown to pieces, so long as there were men to help and wounds to heal.

When the St. Antoine closed I took her to the American Consulate to find a house where she could stay. That night and the next loads of English Red Cross busses with their households of pain and ether rumbled over the pontoon bridge across the Scheldt, went past Fort Tete de Flandre, and disappeared in the swampy meadows on the road to Ghent. I never saw her again, but I have always hoped that Mrs. Richardson was among the nurses who went with them.

When on Wednesday morning I was turned out of my room, I made my way past a pressing throng of foreign faces to the Queen's Hotel on the water front. There I found Arthur Ruhl and James H. Hare, who had just come over from England. The hotel overlooked the River Scheldt, forming a wide crescent on the city's north, and was within fifty yards of one of the longest pontoon bridges constructed in modern warfare.

Here was a sight to come again and rend the memory. The crowds were endeavoring to get away over one of the two avenues of escape still open. I estimated that between five in the afternoon and the following dawn three hundred thousand persons must have passed through the city's gates. They were the people of Antwerp itself, swelled by exiles from Alost, Aerschot, Malines, Termonde, and other cities to the south and west. Intermittently for two days and nights I watched them from my room in the Queen's. From five yards beneath my window ledge came the shuffle, shuffle of unending feet, the creak and groans of heavy cart wheels, the talk and babble of guttural tongues, the yelp of hounds, as the thousands moved and wept and surged and jostled along throughout the night and into the uncertain mist of that October morning. They were so close I could have jumped into their carts or dropped a pebble on their heads. Infinitely more impressive than the retreat of the allied armies or the victorious entry of the Germans a little later, was the pageant of this pitiful army without guns or leaders.

The twenty-foot entrance to that pontoon bridge seemed to me like the mouth of a funnel through which poured the dense misery of an entire nation. Think of this army's composition: a great city was emptying itself of human life; not only a great city, but all the people driven to it from the outside, all who had congregated in Belgium's last refuge and its strongest fort. They bore themselves bravely, the greater number plodding along silently in the footsteps of those who went ahead, with no thoughts of their direction, some of them even chatting and laughing. You saw great open wagons carrying baby carriages, perambulators, pots and kettles, an old chair, huge bundles of household goods, and the ubiquitous Belgian bicycle strapped to the side. There were small wagons, and more great wagons crowded with twenty, thirty, forty people: aged brown women, buried like shrunk walnuts in a mass of shawls, girls sitting listlessly on piles of straw, and children fitfully asleep or very much awake and crying lustily.

Sometimes the men and boys mounted their bicycles, rode for a dozen yards, were stopped by the procession, and then, for want of better occupation, rang their bells. One saw innumerable yelping dogs: big Belgian police hounds harnessed to the cart and doing their share of work, others sniffing along the outskirts and plainly advertising for an owner. There were noisy cattle, too, some of which escaped. Long after the city was evacuated I saw a cow bellowing under an archway of the Cathedral of Notre Dame.

In this way the city emptied itself, but so slowly that the very slowness of the movement wore the marchers out. Each family group was limited to the speed of its oldest member. Hundreds gave it up and lay by the road, or formed little gypsy camps under the trees. At night these were lighted by fires, overshadowed by the greater fire from the distant burning city, and beside them stretched dumb-looking souls, watching vaguely those who still had strength to move.

Watching these wretches got so on my nerves that I had to get out and do something. With a British intelligence officer, formerly of Sir John French's staff, I wandered down to the southern quarter of the city known as Berchem. As usual, the guns at the outer forts had been booming throughout the evening. From the city's ramparts you could not only feel the shudder of the earth, but you could see occasional splashes of flame from the Belgian batteries, answered, in the dim distance to the south, by smaller, less vivid splashes issuing from the mouths of the German instruments of "Culture" which throughout the night pounded ruthlessly on the unprotected houses without the city limits.

On the way home we stopped in at the British field hospital to see a wounded British friend.

Chapter VI

The Surrender Of Antwerp

As we left the British field hospital, on the Rue de Leopold, a shrieking skyrocket whizzed by above us and buried its hissing head in the river to the north. One or two more fell at a distance of several hundred yards, and in the southern part of the city flames from several houses shot up into the quiet, windless night.

The bombardment was on—the time was 12.07 Wednesday midnight.

For a moment I did not realize that this was the beginning of the end of Antwerp. I had heard so much gun-fire and seen so many bombs dropping from aeroplanes that I did not fully appreciate the significance of these shells. I scribbled a few notes in my diary, unstrapped my money belt, and then picked out an empty bed at the Queen's Hotel and tumbled in. I must have slept for six or seven hours.

When I arose everything was quiet. The hotel was apparently deserted. I remember being particularly irritated because there was no one in the kitchen who would give me breakfast, so I made myself some tea and then strolled into the street. It so happened that the Germans had been pumping lead steadily into the city for six hours and that this was the morning lull. The Germans are methodical in everything. When they bombard a city they stop for breakfast.

As I walked down the Avenue de Keyser I thought at first it was Sunday—or rather a year of Sundays all rolled into one. Overnight the city had been transformed into a tomb. Shops were closed; iron shutters were pulled down everywhere; trolley cars stood in the street as they had been left. My own footsteps resounded fearfully on the pavement, and I walked five blocks before I saw a human being.

I stopped at the American Consul's office on the Place de Meir, only to find the place was locked. A frightened face behind the grating told me that the consul had taken his wife to the country — good place to be in, I thought.

Things began to seem lonely. I heard shells falling and saw flames in the southern quarter of the city, and decided to go in that direction to look up an American correspondent and two photographers who had asked me to bunk with them in the cellar of a little abandoned house at 74 Rue de Peage.

Turning down a little side street leading toward the Boulevard de Leopold, I was greeted by a clap of thunder overhead. A shell demolished a house across the street and about thirty yards down. The concussion knocked over a couple of babies. I picked them up, put them back in the doorway of the house where they seemed to belong, saying over and over again mechanically, "There, there, don't cry. There is nothing to be frightened about"; and then, just to show how little I myself was frightened I began to run. I ran for all I was worth. I ran right into the fire. The shells were falling fairly thick on the Boulevard de Leopold; every two or three hundred yards a house was partially destroyed; bricks and glass littered the pavement, and occasionally, every quarter of a mile or so, I saw a figure skulking along under the eaves of a building, crouching and ducking in time to the nasty music of the shells. But I decided that the middle of the street was the safest part.

When I had gone about a quarter of a mile I got my nerve again. I put my hands in my pockets, lighted a cigarette, and was just saying to myself, "This is pretty good fun, after all," when CRASH!! CRASH!! two, or possibly three, shells, bursting in rapid succession, tore down houses a hundred yards ahead of me. Then one struck in the street, and jagged fragments of angry shrapnel skidded along the pavement like a thrown stone skipping along the surface of the water. I was again trembling all over.

Was the game worth the candle, I asked myself. "I've come three thousand miles and overcome every obstacle just to get into this horrible mess. If I get disfigured — no, I'd much rather be killed — will it — "

"Crash!! Bang!!" went a monster shell as I turned the corner.

Two doors from the corner of a narrow street covered with bricks and mortar fluttered a United States flag, and beneath it the door of 74 Rue de Peage. This place was later spoken of as "Thompson's fort," because Donald C. Thompson, a Kansas photographer, took possession of it after the Belgian family fled, and plundered the neighborhood for coffee, rolls, and meat, with which he stocked his little cellar. The house next door had already been struck, and shattered glass littered the pavement. The doorstep of 74 was covered by a couple of mattresses and sand-bags. Beneath this, in a dingy sort of coal-bin, heaped with straw, I found crouching the tenants of "Thompson's fort."

Next to Berchem, the southern quarter of the city, where the Germans were approaching, the Rue de Peage was the worst spot in Antwerp. We sat for a time listening to the shells. There were here, in
addition to Thompson, Edwin Weigel, a Chicago photographer; Edward Eyre Hunt, of "Collier's Weekly"; and the Dutch Vice-Consul.

We heard the distant resounding Boom … Boom … Boom … ed … Boom … Boom … Boom.

An interval of perhaps a second's silence, then a faint moaning, a crescendo wail, the whirr and rush of a snarling, shrieking skyrocket overhead, and a crash, like all the thunders of the universe rolled into one, when the shell struck, followed by the roar of falling brick as a neighboring house came pouring into the street.

"Whee…..wheee…..Hi…..HIOU UIOUW," we heard. "Whee … whEEE … whEEE … UIOUW … OUWW … SSH … SSHSHHH … BANG … BANG!!!!!!"

"Whee…..wheee…..Hi…..HIOUUIOUW," we heard. "Whee … whEEE … whEEE … UIOUW… OUWW… SSH … SSHSHHH… BANG… BANG!!!!!!"

I tried to persuade the other fellows to come up to the Queen's Hotel along the Scheldt waterfront on the northern side of the city, where I was then encamped. It was a safer locality because the Germans had not yet got the range of the northern end of the city.

Weigel and Thompson, having to look out for their kodaks and moving-picture paraphernalia, decided to wait a while, as did Hunt. Hare, who came in later, had two big kodaks which he wanted to get back to his room in the Queen's. I offered to carry one of them for him.

We shook hands all around and one or two of us exchanged messages to be taken back in case there was any trouble—that is to say, in case, as seemed likely at the time, some of us should get out alive and some should not. Hunt gave me a letter to his family, and later, with watch in hand, started to walk around the burning city to calculate the number of falling shells per minute! I slung Hare's kodak over my shoulder and we started back, taking separate streets. It was a dash of three quarters of a mile and nothing fell particularly close to us, although the buildings on all sides were in flames. Near a pile of discarded uniforms of the garde civique, I saw what was left of the figure of a man with his insides oozing out, his eyes still open, staring vacantly upwards, and all around him the horrible odor of decaying horses. By this time I was calm and was getting quite accustomed to the bursting of shells. I suppose I had been through my "baptism of fire."

About half an hour later, when we were sitting in the Queen's, Thompson, pale as a sheet, staggered into the deserted lobby closely followed by Weigel and Hunt and the Dutch Vice-Consul, the latter somewhat out of his head. Just after I left 74 Rue de Peage, a 32 cm. shell burst on the roof, tearing off the two top floors of the house, throwing Thompson's bed into the street, and setting the place on fire. At sundown the house was in ashes. Somehow or other the men all got out, rescuing a portion of their paraphernalia.

All Thursday afternoon the German Taubes circled above the city— mostly along the waterfront. Below them puffed little clouds of smoke where shells from the Belgian anti-aircraft guns were exploding. I fancy the airmen were locating the pontoon bridge and signaling to the Prussian battery commanders six miles away; but during Wednesday and Thursday, when the crowds of refugees were assembled on the waterfront, not a single bomb dropped among them. A few shells, well placed, would have slaughtered them like sheep. Before and during the bombardment I am quite certain that the Germans intended to frighten, rather than injure, non-combatants. Report to the contrary notwithstanding, it is equally true that, so far as possible, the invaders kept to their promise to spare such buildings as the Cathedral, the Palais de Justice, the Hotel de Ville, the Castle Steen, and other historic landmarks.

The bombardment lasted forty hours. That night, — Thursday, October 8th, — the second and last night which the town held out, all of the Americans who were left gathered at the Queen's. The firing by this time was terrific. Except for the lurid glare of the burning buildings which lit up the streets, the city was in total darkness. For weeks martial law had been in effect and there were no lights after sundown. An unearthly feeling it was, to be locked in the darkness of this strange city, unable to speak a word of the language, not knowing whether the garrison had evacuated the forts or whether the city had been surrendered, believing there would be street righting or an insurrection of franc-tireurs. At times we heard through the darkness the tramp of squads of soldiers. Surely, we thought, there come the Germans. We remembered the atrocities at Louvain.

About an hour after darkness settled on us I climbed to the roof of the Queen's Hotel, from which, for a few minutes, I looked out upon the most horrible and at the same time the most gorgeous panorama that I ever hope to see. The entire southern portion of the city appeared a desolate ruin; whole streets were ablaze, and great sheets of fire rose to the height of thirty or forty feet.

The night, like the preceding, was calm and quiet, without a breath of wind. On all sides rose greedy tongues of flame which seemed to thirst for things beyond their reach. Slowly and majestically the sparks floated skyward; and every now and then, following the explosion of a shell, a new burst of flame lighted up a section hitherto hidden in darkness. The window panes of the houses still untouched flashed the reflection in our eyes.

Even more glorious was the scene to the north. On the opposite side of the Scheldt the oil tanks, the first objects to be set on fire by bombs from the German Taubes, were blazing furiously and vomiting huge volumes of oil-laden smoke. Looking over on this side of the river, too, I could see the crackling wooden houses of the village of St. Nicolas, lighting with their glow all of northern Antwerp and the water-front. In the swampy meadows on the farther bank we could see the frightened refugees as they hurried along the still protected road to Ghent. They passed on our side of the burning village, not five hundred yards away. Every now and then as a fitful flame lighted the meadow I could see the figures silhouetted against the red background.

They appeared to be actually walking through the flames like Shadrach, Meshach, and Abednego. It was all a glorious and fascinating nightmare.

There was at this time an ominous lull in the moaning pound of shrapnel.

Out of the darkness in the direction of West Antwerp came a new sound-the low methodical beat of feet. The noise became gradually louder and louder until one could hear the rumble of heavy wheels and distinguish the sound of voices above the crowd. This was the beginning of the British and Belgian retreat, which started at about eight o'clock Thursday night, and, under cover of darkness, continued unbroken for eight hours. Following the line taken by the escaping populace this retreat went past our position on the water-front. Before dawn on Friday morning, when the light became strong enough for the advancing army to make out the enemy's position, practically the entire Belgian army plus ten thousand Royal British Naval Marines had got across the pontoon bridge and were well along the road to Ghent. During all these hours squads of gendarmes with fixed bayonets held back such remaining townsfolk as attempted to get near the bridge. To these wretches it seemed that their last avenue of escape had been cut off. There were now at the Queen's, Arthur Ruhl, Hare, and myself, in addition to an English intelligence officer and the recruits from "Fort Thompson." We talked over our plans for the next day. The intelligence officer volunteered to get up with me at sunrise and scour the river for a barge. It was my idea, in case we could make any kind of arrangements for a get-away, to come back and report to the other fellows. I remember that Arthur Ruhl was uncertain as to whether he would come with us or wait for the German entry. He was worried about some friends in the British field hospital, and he decided not to leave without looking them up,—a pretty white thing to do, it seemed to me.

I tried to sleep, but the rumble of artillery wagons and shouts of the marchers prevented. So I spent most of the night of the British and Belgian retreat beneath my window. At daybreak the intelligence officer came to my room and we started out along the waterfront, moving in the direction of the Dutch border. With the rising sun on Friday morning the German Taubes again swept over the city. When the Germans saw that the whole British and Belgian army had got away from them they moved up their 42 cm. guns and literally gave us hell. This time they had no mercy on the few remaining noncombatants.

The intelligence officer's baggage delayed us a long time. When we got up nearly as far as Fort St. Philippe, we separated. We saw a barge anchored in the river and he had an idea it would leave about seven o'clock, and that we might be able to get on it. I gave him my knapsack containing my gold belt, which, in the confusion, I had not had time to strap on, and started to make a dash back to the Queen's, because I considered that I ought to let the other fellows know what had happened to us.

I had fifteen minutes to cover the distance.

I ran. The shells, at that time, were falling at a rate, I should judge, of five a minute. Opposite the Castle Steen I had a narrow escape—just concussion, I suppose. Directly above me came a crash of thunder. A few moments later I found myself lying in the street, head pointing north—dazed. A bomb crashed through the eaves and tore a hole as big as a small cellar in the street directly before the old castle, bursting with the concussion of a tornado. For a few moments I sat on the street feeling weak in the legs and unable to move.

Again I started back to the Queen's. Two hundred yards east of the bridge some soldiers held me up.

"Get back!" they shouted, believing that I was making for the pontoon. They turned me back, and I hesitated a moment. A terrible explosion, louder than anything I had yet heard, rocked the city to its foundations. For a moment the walls of the houses trembled and every window on the waterfront was broken. The retreating Belgian army had blown up that pontoon bridge and with it what then seemed the last hope of escape for the few remaining survivors. For a few moments wreckage writhed in midstream like a great sea creature in agony of death.

Past me rushed groups of Belgian soldiers, the remainder of a few hundred who had been left to cover the British and Belgian retreat, fire the last shots from the forts, and spike the guns as the Germans approached. Pitiable was the terror of these fellows when they saw the bridge gone. Many of them were out of their heads through exposure and exhaustion; not a few of them wept. One sergeant tore off his uniform and fatigue cap and tried to exchange them for my citizen's clothes.

The worst fire of the entire bombardment was concentrated during these moments; the racket was stupendous. Because gunboats, barges, lighters, tenders, rowboats, were commandeered by the military authorities to ferry across soldiers and wounded there was slim chance for noncombatants. Above the noise of bomb and shrapnel Belgian gunboats added to the confusion by cannonading big boats along the quay. This was done in order that the Germans might not make use of them for the pursuit. It speaks volumes for my military knowledge that for a brief moment I imagined the Germans had embarked upstream and were going to make a river battle of it.

By this time the American correspondents had left the Queen's, going in different directions for different purposes. Hunt and Thompson, I later learned, went to the American Consulate, where they stayed during the German entry.

For a moment I see-sawed up and down the river bank, remembering I had left my handbag at the Queen's, but, infinitely more important, that my knapsack with money belt and diary were in the keeping of a peripatetic acquaintance somewhere along the crowded piers downstream. Without that gold, the thousands of miles to New York seemed doubly long. When I at last got back to the barge office a dock-hand pointed to a bench in the corner; there to my intense relief lay the knapsack, where my kind English intelligence officer had left it.

A little later I managed to clamber on a river barge laden nearly to the sinking point with Antwerp's peaceful burghers and their dumb-looking women and children. Slowly—very slowly—we steamed out of the haze of powder and oil-laden smoke, through long lines of gunboats and a flotilla of drifting scows packed to the gunwales like our own, and past Fort St. Philippe, whose garrison were at that moment heaving tons of powder into the river.

A few miles farther downstream they landed us on the northern bank of the Scheldt near the little town of Liefkenshack. Here I began a few miles of walking, occasionally varied by ox-cart locomotion.

I was traveling with nothing but a knapsack (my suitcase had to be abandoned) and therefore moving faster than the crowd. At one point, for the sake of company, I joined a group and took a turn at shoving the family wheel-barrow. They poured out thanks in the guttural Flemish tongue, then loaded me with bread and bits of mouldy pie. When that was not accepted they feared for their hospitality. They talked and I talked, with a result that was hardly worth the effort. Finally, after a conference, one of the group disappeared into the crowd and returned leading an eight-year-old boy.

"Me talk American," said the boy. "We two speak together?"

And so we talked, for the road was long and weary.

Their advance was so gradual that, although I did not leave Antwerp until the bombardment was over, I caught up with the army of refugees before Roosendaal, just across the Dutch border.

Here Holland opened out her arms. The kindness of the Dutch—as yet personal, unorganized endeavor—was beyond conception.

Churches, houses, public halls, stations were thrown open to the multitude. You saw hundreds of Dutch soldiers join in the procession, lift babies and bundles, and walk with them for miles. At Dordrecht, when the trains came through, peasants passed scores of babies' milk-bottles into the cars. When a jolly-looking Dutch girl, with a great big gleaming smile that reminded me of some one, gave me milk and chocolate, the tears began to trickle down my cheeks. I suppose it was the reaction, or because I was tired, or, perhaps, because the crowd was cheering and waving at us. For the others there were piles of bread, Dutch cake, and, best of all, some good, long drinks of water. For ten days Antwerp's water supply had been cut off. Von Beseler, German siege commander, had seen to that.

At Bergen op Zoom and Roosendaal people used the walls of the houses for post-offices. They wrote their names in chalk letters, giving directions to relatives lost in the scramble.

After ox carts, rowboats, and river barges had done their share, a Dutch-Belgian "Stoom Tram" joggled us along for a few miles. Some more walking and a little running before I at last crawled aboard a twenty-car freight and passenger train moving slowly toward the east.

At the first telegraph office across the Dutch border, I filed a cable story to the "Boston Journal"; and later started an account for the "New York Evening Post." I had an idea that I would score a "beat" or "scoop" so that the people of the Back Bay could read of Antwerp's fall over their coffee-cups the next morning. My cable account had too much inside information. There were in it too many facts concerning Winston Churchill's visit, also information about the number of Royal Marines engaged, none of which it was thought proper to give out at that time. So the English censor refused to let it through. That, however, did not prevent the Dutch Cable Company from pocketing my two hundred guilders.

By the time I reached Rotterdam the word "refugee" had assumed a new and altogether nearer meaning. I had been in a besieged and captured city; I had mixed with homeless and starving people; I had seen houses crumble and burn; and ghastly human figures with their insides oozing away and the eyes staring vacantly.

As I lay in bed that night I could hear, and I still can hear, the scruff, scruff, and shuffle of feet as the compact body of this army — the army without guns or leaders — dragged slowly past my window at the Queen's, the tinkle of ox-cart bells, the talk and babble of guttural tongues; the curses of the team drivers, the frantic cries of mothers who had lost their children in the scramble, the cries of young children who didn't know what was wrong, but realized in their vague, childish way that something terrible was happening.

I could see, and I still can see, those big Belgian hounds sniffing along the outskirts of the crowd and plainly advertising for an owner; I can see other hounds with their heads thrown back wailing at the door of their deserted and abandoned homes. And I can see the Dutch border where Holland opened out her arms, and the Dutch peasants gave us rye bread and sandwiches and good long drinks of welcome milk.

Sometimes I can sit with my legs dangling over the stern of that old towboat barge on which I finally made my escape, and can visualize the blue-gray spire of the Cathedral of Notre Dame, standing, it seemed to me, a quiet sentinel over the ruins of the tortured city; and, then, as the old barge sweeps around the river's bend, I can look back upon the last of Antwerp's story written in flaming letters of red against the early morning sky.

Chapter VII

Spying On Spies

Less than forty-eight hours after the fall of Antwerp the wave of helpless humanity whose crest broke on the Belgian border had rolled over the entire length and breadth of Holland. Thousands of Belgian refugees wandered as far north as The Hague, where various Dutch relief committees and the American Legation at The Hague did their best to house the homeless and relieve the suffering. Dr. van Dyke rolled up his sleeves still farther and strained to solve the problem of the unemployed, sometimes, when a case interested him, turning his own pocket inside out.

Eight days after the Antwerp bombardment, I left The Hague for my second trip into Germany.

Just before my start Captain Sunderland, U.S.A., at the head of the American Relief Committee at The Hague, asked me to help him in taking charge of two carloads of grain, which were to go across the German border and be distributed among the starving Belgians at Liege. England had agreed not to interfere with food supplies, provided the United States saw that they did not fall into German hands in Belgium. The present job required sleeping in the freight cars and saying, in one form or another, "Hands off!" to every spiked helmet that tried to interfere. Captain Sunderland could speak no German, and as I had already been over the same territory and had had some experience with the military authorities, he wished me to accompany him.

I decided, however, to go into the interior of Germany. I had already seen three armies in the field, and had watched, more or less closely, the people of two warring nations. I was now particularly anxious to study the German point of view, and if possible get to the front with the Crown Prince's army.

For such a purpose I considered that I carried good enough credentials. In addition to a packet of mail for Ambassador Gerard, my letter from ex-President Roosevelt, and my United States passport, which had been vised by Herr von Mueller, German Ambassador at The Hague, I now carried a special laissez-passer which Mr. Marshall Langhorne had been kind enough to secure for me from the same legation. I had a letter from Count von Bernstorff, whom I had seen the night he arrived in America, and a letter from Herr von Biel, Secretary of the German Embassy at The Hague, recommending me to the Foreign Office in Berlin. Professor Hugo Munsterberg had taken the trouble to send me a note to Dr. R. W. Drechsler, head of the American Institute in Berlin, and I had also a letter to the head of the University of Berlin.

It was a five-hours' run from The Hague to Bentheim, a small country village on the German frontier. The train stopped a quarter of a mile north of the border. Dutch officials came aboard to examine passports and baggage of every passenger. They were good-natured and talkative, and did not go minutely into details, as those leaving the country were less carefully watched than "immigrants." Me, however, they mistook for an Englishman (as was usually the case in Germany) and told me I could not cross the frontier. A Dutch manufacturer, with whom I had struck up an acquaintance, explained my identity, and the official, who looked astonished, waved me ahead with a doubtful expression, as much as to say, "On your own head be it, young man."

That first night passed without trouble. At the border station we lined up, immigrant fashion, and went through an inspection by a number of the businesslike German militariat attached to the Zollamt, or customs service. For ten minutes I stood in suspense while a fiery-looking officer, with a snapping blue eye, looked through my credentials in silence. He wrote my name in a notebook, looked through my eye as if he would read my very soul, and then, without a remark, passed me on. I filed through a narrow gate — and so into the Realms of the Kaiser.

It was now eleven o'clock at night and the Berlin express came through Bentheim at 7.45 the next morning. We stayed at a little inn, somewhat resembling the Wayside Inn, at Sudbury, Massachusetts.

Here I fell in with a German manufacturer whom I had seen several weeks before as we were bringing the good news from Ghent to Aix. I was surprised at this man's change of opinion regarding the conflict. On the first occasion he laughed outright at the idea of an extended fight. Now, all through his arguments, he repeated such phrases as, "Well, if Germany doesn't win," or, "Suppose the war does last two years," etc., etc.

In the morning I had a peculiarly disagreeable experience at Lohne, some distance from the German frontier, where we had again to change trains en route to the capital. Experience had by this time taught me, when thrown with people on the road, to show them my papers and make my identity known as soon as possible.

I therefore clung pretty closely to my argumentative German acquaintance of Bentheim and Aix. During the melee of changing cars I was, however, separated from him, and became engaged in conversation (spoken in English) with a Dutch chocolate merchant. The argument must have been interesting, for I did not at first notice a crowd of twenty or thirty travelers and villagers gathering around us: I did, however, notice when they began to push and jostle in a manner obviously intended for insult. When I tried to retreat the exits were locked. The crowd, convinced that I was an English spy, closed more compactly and manhandled me off toward an officer on the street behind the platform. My hat was knocked off, and for a brief moment I recalled the lynching anger which I had seen in the eyes of Belgian mobs, as German spies in Antwerp were being led to the police station.

At the last moment my rescuer came in the shape of the German friend of Bentheim, who broke through the mob and whispered in my ear, "Speak German. Always speak in German, you fool!"

I admitted the soft impeachment.

"Ich bin ein Amerikaner—ein correspondent," I explained to the row of angry faces; and while my German friend soothed and reassured his testy compatriots, I moved away, glad enough to escape another visit to jail. Those personally conducted jail tours were not so bad, I had found, with a handsome gendarme at your side; but a howling crowd was altogether another matter.

I reached the capital that night. One of my letters says, a few days later: —

"The atmosphere is oppressive to the Anglo-Saxon visitor. His looks, his manner, his accent betray him as one of the English-speaking pest, and the crowd, with its mind so full of English hatred, does not readily distinguish the American. So drop into a word of English in a cafe: your neighbor glowers and draws away. You face it out with a nonchalant air, but gradually the tension grows, especially when, as happened to-day at the prisoners' camp at Zossen, twenty miles south of Berlin, a great burly Prussian puts a menacing eye on you and says, without introduction: 'It is very dangerous for an Englishman here!'

"Day by day here the hatred grows of England and things English: judging from the press and the temper of the people, one would think that England is the only foe. As a nation and as individuals they bear no particular malice toward France. They even feel sorry for 'misguided' Belgium—betrayed by the British, they say. But England they look upon as the root of all their trouble, the despicable, retreating enemy they cannot touch, the enemy, they maintain, whose clever, but selfish, diplomacy has forced the brunt of the fighting on the others, while she sits back to wait for the spoils."

On my arrival in Berlin I delivered the mail packet to Ambassador Gerard. Two days later I presented my credentials at the Auswartige Amt, or Foreign Office, hoping to get permission to go to the western front with the Crown Prince's army. I was told to see Baron von Mumm Schwartzenstein, who was officially designated by Von Jagow to handle neutral correspondents, and who, unofficially, I have reason to believe, is connected with the Secret Service. He is a pudgy sort of man, with a watery skin, and decidedly not of military build or bearing. When, after much red tape, I was finally admitted to an outer office, he stepped out to see me, merely taking my name and the names of the papers I represented. I was told to come back in the evening. When I did so and was admitted to His Holy of Holies, he said to me at once: —

"I was expecting you to come yesterday. Why did you not?"

This was rather startling, but his next remark altogether took away my breath.

"Were you satisfied with your treatment by the War Office in Brussels, Herr Green? And why, if you have already been wiss ze army in scenes of war, do you now come to me for permission?"

Mind you, I had at this time spoken scarcely a word, and had certainly told nothing of my age or previous condition of servitude in Brussels. But the Government that never forgets knew all about my movements. He smiled at my discomfiture, and, within the next few minutes, proved to be such a genial German (for war-time) that I soon told him all about my adventures, including the fact that I had gone back into Antwerp and entered Belgian lines, after escaping from German surveillance at Aix. I happened to speak of the marvelous efficiency and preparedness of the German army in Belgium.

"Yes, that iss quite so," remarked His Excellency, with a smile. "You see, we were prepared for everysing—except," he added after a pause,—"except ze invasion of ze American newspaperman. When he iss out of our sight, zen we do not feel secure."

Several weeks later, after I had come out of the Kaiser's realm, a representative of the "Boston Journal," who had been looking for me all over the Continent, ran me down just as I was leaving The Hague for England.

"The Foreign Office in Berlin told me where to find you," he said. "They told me that in Berlin you had stayed first at the Esplanade, and then you had moved to the Kaiserhof. They said you had left the city [this was when I went out toward Poland], that you had returned to Berlin, and that on such and such a date at 8.45 you had departed for The Hague."!!

The military and civil authorities looked upon the correspondent as an embryo spy. And if the correspondent's sympathies were foreign, he was a thousand times worse than the ordinary spy, because he could make use of the cable and press to spread his information.

While waiting in Berlin for a chance to go to the front, I became, therefore, more and more conscious of surveillance. Whether it was the fact of being so much alone, or due perhaps to an unfortunately English-like appearance, I do not know. At all events, the long arm of the Secret Service continuously cast a shadow over my shoulder: I even became suspicious of myself.

For one who has not been through the experience it is difficult to appreciate the strain of such constant, unending suspicion. On July 17,1912, I stood beside the body of Herman Rosenthal, the gambler, as it lay in the coffin in the parlor of his house in the Tenderloin. My newspaper had sent me to "cover" the funeral, and I managed, because of some previous knowledge of the household, and by giving the impression of a mourner, to gain access. The murderers had not yet been caught. Because the public knew nothing of "Lefty" Louie, or "Gyp the Blood," or even of the late Lieutenant Becker, it was common gossip that the criminals lurked in the neighborhood, and that, in order to avoid suspicion, they would appear among the chief mourners. Therefore, each eye was turned against its neighbor, and each man, as he passed you, asked the silent question, — "Did you shoot Herman Rosenthal?" During all the months on the Continent, and particularly in Germany, I felt myself at Rosenthal's funeral.

To a greater or less degree other correspondents had similar experiences. I must mention one or two of them, in spite of the fact that they may dim the importance of my own adventures. There was Swing, of Chicago, German by relationship and sympathy, who championed the Kaiser's cause and in his dispatches blew the Teuton horn in the Middle West of America. Swing was given exceptional privileges, including a typewriter and telephone near the Foreign Office. Yet Swing himself was constantly shadowed, and it is a fact that every time he used the telephone (and he was never permitted to speak in English) a Secret Service agent cut in on the wire to listen to the conversation.

An anecdote which I have heard in connection with the same correspondent, although I do not vouch for its accuracy, shows that "keeping the lid" on newspaper men had its humorous side. It likewise indicates the initiative and aggressiveness of many American correspondents, who, as a rule, went right ahead in the face of military regulations, in some cases risking their lives, and in almost every case refusing to be "bluffed out," even where the threatened penalty was death. Swing had made his way to the battle front near—- — —-, where he was taken into custody and brought before Von Mumm, then on a visit to Staff Headquarters.

"I find one of your countrymen wizin ze army lines," is the way Excellency von Mumm is reported as telling the story, "and I say to him, 'Herr Swing, it iss strongly forbidden zat a newspaper man come to ze front. It is not permitted zat any one come here; you must go away.'

"Very goot, Excellency," said Swing.

"Ze next day I am extr-r-remely sorry to encounter ze same chen-tleman, and I say to him, 'Go away at once. If you are not gone in one hour you will be shot!'

"Very goot, Excellency," answered Herr Swing. "Auf wiedersehn."

"Zat Very afternoon, to my sur-r-r-prise and gr-r-reat astonish-ment, I see him again. He was still in ze army lines. And I say to him, 'Now I have you! This time you will be shot at sunrise!'

"And he look at me and say:—

"'Very goot, Excellency. Zat make perfectly bully story for my pa-per.'

"And I look at him for a minute, and I do not know whether to shoot him or to laugh.

"And you know, I cannot help myself but to laugh."

And finally there was the case of Cyril Brown, staff correspond-ent of the "New York Times" in Berlin, with whom I floundered through the maze of official red tape and military snares that entan-gled the reporter at the German capital. Brown is an individual with a sense of humor and a Mark Twain penchant for ten-pfennig ci-gars. He takes his work seriously, but, unlike most war correspond-ents, not himself. After some interesting freight-car adventures of his own planning, he reached the Grosser Hauptquartier, a small city on the Meuse, where at that time the brain of the German fighting machine was located. This most vulnerable spot of the en-tire German Empire was, paradoxically, in France. The Kaiser, the King of Saxony, the Crown Prince of Germany, and Field Marshal von Moltke were here holding council of war. It was therefore of utmost importance to conceal the locality. Neutral correspondents were not allowed: the German press, even if it knew, would not dare to breathe its whereabouts. When Brown by strategy got inside the red-and-white striped poles which marked the entrance to the Over War Lord's quarters, he was at once arrested and taken before Major Nikolai, head of the Kaiser's bodyguard and chief of the field detectives.

It was late at night, and it was determined that Brown should go on the first military Postzug, which left at 7 A.M. If he was not gone by that time there were terrible threats of what would happen to him.

It so happened that the day was the Crown Princess's birthday. Soldiers, grenadiers, and servants of the Kaiser's household celebrated the fact. Brown evaded his intoxicated sentinels and deliberately missed the train. The following morning Major Nikolai discovered him behind the guardhouse, himself feigning intoxication. Major Nikolai was about to throw Brown into jail "for the duration of the war" when the young man answered:—

"But, Major, I overslept. What loyal German could possibly remain sober on the Crown Princess's birthday?"

"Gott im Himmel!" exclaimed the major, bursting into a laugh; "vatever can be done mit such a man?"

To-day Brown has free run of the Foreign Office and the War Office in Berlin, and is sending to his paper, in my humble opinion, the best information obtainable in this country on the way in which the German civil and military mind views the "crisis" with the U. S. A.

Chapter VIII

The Sorrow Of The People

I was conscious of a distinct break between the crisp, official atmosphere of Berlin—where the war hurts least and the mechanical appearance of success is strong—and the sentiment of the rank and file of people whose suffering, as the war continued, became a more and more important factor.

On the night of my second arrival in the capital I sat in the rear of a motion-picture theater, just off the Friedrichstrasse. It was a long, dark hallway, such as one may see in any of the cheaper "movies" on Washington Street or Broadway, where the audience sits in silence broken by the whirr of the cinematograph and in darkness pierced by the flickering light upon the screen. The woman in the seat beside mine was the typical Hausfrau of the middle class. She was, of course, dressed in mourning: the heavy veil, which was thrown back, revealed the expression so common to the German widow of to-day —that set, defiant look which begs no pity, and seems to say: "We've lost them once; we 'd endure the same torture again if we had to."

It was a sad enough story that the reel clicked off, and about as melodramatic as "movies" usually are. But the woman kept herself well in hand, since the public display of grief is forbidden and they who sorrow must sorrow alone.

A Bavarian boy, as I recall it,—the youngest son,—runs away from home to join his father's regiment in Poland. When his captain calls for volunteers for a dangerous mission, the boy steps forward. For hours they trudge over the snow until surrounded by a Cossack patrol. The Bavarian boy, although having a chance to escape, goes back under fire to succor his wounded comrade. Just as he is about to drag the comrade into the zone of safety, a bullet pierces his lung.

For two days he suffers torture on the snow. The body is found and brought home to his mother.

Now and then the widow next me bit her lip and clenched her fist, but she gave no other sign of emotion. Another film was thrown on the screen, humorous, I believe. Suddenly the woman began to laugh. She did not stop laughing. It was a long, mirthless, dry, uncanny sort of cackle. People stared. She laughed still louder. An usher came down the aisle, and stood there, uncertain what to do. Hysterics had given way to weeping: the tears were now streaming down the woman's face. She tried to control herself, but could not, and then arose and between choking sobs and laughter fled from the darkened room out into the Friedrichstrasse.

I mention this incident—the sort of thing that must have existed everywhere, if one had eyes to see it—merely because it gave a glimpse through the veil of public optimism into the wells of sorrow hidden for the sake of public duty. Military and official Berlin was "staged," one might almost say. It was on show to impress the neutral stranger, no less than its own inhabitants, with the glorious sense of victory.

But beneath it lay untold suffering which could be endured only because of such united loyalty and team play as the world has seldom seen.

This undercurrent of suffering, which increased week by week as the writing on the wall grew longer, was in pitiful contrast to the enthusiasm with which the women sent their men and sons away to war. More than once I watched troops drilling at Spandau Hof, the great barracks and training-grounds, a few kilometers west of the city. When, on the evening of my first visit, a half dozen battalions of Landwehr, just whipped into shape, entrained for the front, the people threw bits of earth upon them, and, according to custom, stuck green twigs in the end of every Mauser barrel, that each man might carry a bit of the Vaterland with him on to the enemy's soil. In unspotted field uniforms, and helmets still without the green-gray canvas service covering, they clattered past the reviewing officers, each right leg coming down with the thumping goose-step salute, until halls and barracks echoed with the staccato tread of thousands of hob-nailed boots. The lusty military band blazoned out "Die Wacht am Rhein" and other martial airs, until the creepers began to run up and down your back and you felt a lump rising in your throat. Friends, relatives, widows, mothers already in black for other sons, and more than the usual hurrahing crowd had gathered under the arch leading to the railway track. As the close-locked fours went through the gate, the people broke the ranks and pounded each man on the back, while all the time the crowd was shouting.

I asked my neighbor what they were calling.

A German friend in the group explained: "The people shout 'congratulations!'"

At that moment a Red Cross train returning with twenty carloads of wounded stood on the siding. Scores of bandaged heads and limp arms stuck out of the windows,—these were the slightly wounded, —and even the half-dead figures strapped to the cots turned feebly toward the marching troops. Most of these also waved, and those who were physically able shouted the same words—"Bravo!" "Congratulations!" "Bravo!!"

That is the way after many months of war that the women and children send their men away—no regrets, no holding back. "Good luck! Good work! You've got a chance to die for Germany!!"

Such a spirit, and with it a sincerity of purpose that could only come from the conviction of right, is typical of the rank and file of citizens. It cannot fail to impress the neutral stranger, though he has traveled far in other countries at war and seen and lived with their citizens and soldiers. One was forced to believe that the militarists acted in conformity with the feelings of the whole people, and that this hideous war was not merely the result of personal ambition. Except, of course, among the soldiers the belief was most noticeable among the lower classes. One found it among the peasants, one's neighbor in the day coach, the artisan, the shopkeeper. You might reason with a professor, a doctor, or perhaps an official in the Foreign Office at Berlin. But it was not safe to try it on a sturdy peasant with three sons on the firing line. It was like telling a man his mother is no better than she should be.

From the Log

"Among both fighters and those left at home, there is distinctly less of the matinee hero business than in either England or France. The high official in the civil government who said that the women were the best fighters in the German army was not so far from the truth. The pluck of the women is astonishing. There isn't the slightest display of sorrow or call for sympathy. You see them everywhere in the streets, cafes, and shops of Berlin; not in such great numbers, however, as in the lesser provinces and the smaller towns, where the drain of men is enormously heavier.

"Later: Have been twice to the Casualty List Office, or Information Bureau, where the names of the verwundet und gefallen are posted — column after column, company after company, regiment after regiment of fine black type—nothing more or less than a printer's morgue, crowding into one dark hallway the cemetery of a nation. There were fathers, mothers, brothers, and children quietly and unemotionally scanning the lists. It took me back to the terrible week at the White Star offices, after the Titanic went down. At that time the relatives wept (some of them) and nearly all harangued the officials, asking questions, sending telegrams, begging for news. Here they look for the names of their dead,—that's all,—and then go out without a question. You can't ask questions of a Government! The Titanic lasted a week, and this goes on— God knows how long!

"Had supper with Brown. Later a mother in black and a girl, also in black (the daughter, or daughter-in-law, I should judge), came into the Heiniger (?) Cafe while I was sitting there. For three quarters of an hour they listened to the music, neither of them, I'll swear, speaking a word. Then they paid twenty-five pfennigs for their beer and went out, —still silent,—and the Ober bowed low and very respectfully. I asked the waiter who they were, and he said the woman had that day heard of the death of C... her fourth son. Something like the Bixby woman to whom Lincoln wrote his famous letter. And there must be, literally, thousands of them.

"This people is terribly in earnest,—deluded, of course, with devotion to a false idea, but it is the delusion that spells accomplishment. The country is earnestly and honestly possessed with an Idea, and the idea is that Might is Right. That is the awful pity of it. When will the awakening come?

"Later: To-day I had an interview of three quarters of an hour with Herr Dr. R. W. Drechsler, head of the American Institute, attached to the University of Berlin. To-morrow I hope to see Excellency von Harnach, president of the University of Berlin, to whom I have a letter. Dr. Drechsler was kind, agreeable, extremely interesting. He showed me some New York newspapers—the first real news of the war I have had for weeks. The 'Tribune' and 'Times' had an account of us fellows down in the cellar at Antwerp. Drechsler and I had an interesting argument, and before I left he deluged me with pamphlets and literature for the improvement of my mind and sympathies. Even so he was unlike the average German. As a rule they have attempted to cram their arguments down my throat. These Teutons think they can force you to believe.

"Dr. Drechsler and the proprietor of the Kaiserhof, and, of course, the Foreign Office warned me that it was forbidden to go to the prisoners' camps, either at Zossen or Doeberitz. Some correspondents had been taken on 'personally conducted' tours; but because of misinformation sent out the tours were no longer in vogue. So I thought that I would risk it, without permit, and, wishing to take a swing through rural Germany, I decided to visit the camp at Zossen, twenty-five kilometers south of the capital. When the guards weren't looking, I slipped boxes of cigarettes through the barbed-wire fence to Irish privates, and listened to the talk of captured Cossacks, and watched the British Tommies kicking around a 'soccer' football, squabbling about fouls and penalties, and as much excited about the score as if they were at home on Hampstead Heath."

It was chiefly in my wanderings through rural Germany that I was able to rub elbows with the rank and file of citizens, and to get that barometer of public feeling which Colonel Roosevelt, I believe, has called the barber-shop opinion. I think I am justified in saying that during the winter there were many evidences, too many to be overlooked, that a growing minority, suffering through loss of life and realizing the territorial advantages which are now Germany's, earnestly longed for peace on any reasonable terms. The sooner peace came, they felt, the better would be the strategic position of the Vaterland. Some of this minority, in addition to the women, were business men, or professors, or merchants, or doctors.

It was not far from Hanover, where you change cars for Cologne and Aix- la-Chapelle, dispatching-centers of the troops for the northern line of battle, that the Frankfort doctor in the seat next mine began to talk. He was an oldish man over sixty, dressed in mourning, and careworn. He had been to Berlin, he said, to verify the report of his son's death, and was now headed for Aix, where the body lay.

After Uhlman, the fat merchant, left, we were alone in the second-class compartment, and the doctor got up and shut the door on the noise of Landwehr soldiers singing in the section of the troop train attached behind the car. Presently he showed me two postals from his boy. They were the stereotyped cards allotted to the men on the field: on one side space for the address, on the other side the printed word "well," space for the date (but no locality), and the signature. The third card was a casualty report, signed, probably, by the company captain, with the three printed words "slightly wounded," "wounded," and "severely wounded." The first and last were scratched out, but after the word "wounded" was written, "condition low."

The boy must have held out—because the body was sent to Aix—until well along the homeward Red Cross trip. During the Antwerp bombardment, at Brussels, Liege, and Louvain, I had seen scores of the wounded, and had myself slept on those trains with their households of blood and pain and ether, and their long lines of mail cars, box cars, and converted tram cars fitted with their triple rows of berths, one above another. As the old doctor talked, I could see the wheeled hospitals stealing into the city in the darkness—for the troops go off with bands and holiday accompaniment, but the return is made at dead of night, that the public may not know the human cost.

"We must have peace," the doctor finished, "and we must have it soon. I do not say this because I have lost a son, and I do not say it alone. There are thousands who feel it just as much, but they are afraid to speak what is in their mind. You are a traveler from the great city [Berlin], and you do not know what war means. All you have heard is the talk of fight and victory and glory, and that is all you see if you do not look close. You must live in the smaller cities, must see the villages and farms without men, and you must come with me and see the homes without husband or son." For the third time he interrupted himself to ask:—"You are Amerikaner—yes? And why do you come?"

"To see the war and find out what the German people think."

"Then go home and tell your country what I think and say, and many others like me."

It was not easy to forget his tears and final words as he came up on the platform at Hanover, and, looking around to see that no one overheard, whispered hoarsely: "Fangen sie ihre Propagande an, junger Mann, und Gott starke ihre Bemuhungen"—"Start your peace propaganda, young man, and Heaven help the undertaking."

The southern part of this trip was not without its crop of stories, some humorous, and some atrocious. It was impossible to verify the statement of the Bavarian travelers who boasted of the treatment of English prisoners en route to the detention camp. On one occasion sixty were captured, they said, and only five brought home alive. The Bavarian soldiers guarding them said with a laugh, "But they were tired, so we had to shoot the rest"; and the officer answered with a wink, "What happens to English prisoners need never be reported." One never needed more one's sense of the probabilities.

And there was the good-natured cavalry lieutenant who said the Germans had found a way to keep their prisoners in training. "You see," he explained, "we lock twenty of the 'red-trousers' [Frenchmen] and twenty Englishmen in the same room at night and shut the windows. You know a Frenchman can't stand air, and a Kitchener will die without it. So we stand outside to watch the fun. First a window goes up, and then it goes down, and pretty soon there are growls, grumbles, and oaths. In ten minutes a terrible fight ensues; in half an hour the Frenchmen are badly beaten,—they always are,—and twenty battered English heads come sticking out the window for a breath of air."

And finally there was the Landwehr captain's letter, a thing in keeping with the tales which come across the Polish border. Westward, in Belgium and in France, the fight was modern and of the day. Move eastward from Berlin and you got the mediaeval note. It was not to be found at the English prisoners' camp at Doeberitz, where the Germans stare with infinite contempt and satisfaction at Tommy Atkins behind his triple row of wire gratings. But wander among the thousands of captured Cossacks building their own prisons at the camp at Zossen, hear them muttering "Nichevo"—"this is fate"—"I do not care," and, listening to the stories of their captors, you felt the atmosphere of centuries gone by. One such was called to my attention in the form of a Prussian captain's letter, which was, I believe, published in Berlin. Here is his letter of the war in Poland, not long ago received by relatives. So much as is not private is given as he wrote it:—

"The inhabitants go out of our way like frightened dogs, with childish fear. When they wish to ask a question, they kneel down and kiss the border of our coats, as in the days of the serf system. We are stationed here in Poland, about eight kilometers from the so-called road, in a so-called village far from all civilization. The village consists of a number of tumble-down cottages, with rooms which we should not consider fit for stables for our horses. The rain is streaming down unceasingly, as if Heaven wished to wash away all the sins of the world. Our horses sink into the mud up to their knees.

"We took up our quarters in this village after fifty-four hours' marching, and came just in time to witness the end of a strange and tragic romance. When I was about to open the door of a farm, it was opened from the inside, and a subaltern came out, with a face beaming with satisfaction. He reported that a little while ago he, with a few of his men, partly captured and partly shot down half a company of Russians.

"'We were concealed' he told me. 'We let them come quite near, and then we started firing.'

"We entered a low-ceilinged room, or pen, sparsely lighted by wax candles. The first object which caught my attention was a youthful Russian soldier, almost a child, lying on a straw mattress, smiling as if asleep. I approached; I put my hand on his forehead … ice-cold— dead. Some of the men approached to take off the clothing; others stood around in a half-circle, silently looking on. Suddenly there was a murmur… They seemed awe-stricken, these brave fellows, who are not daunted even by overwhelming odds. They hesitated, and one of them, advancing a few paces to me, reports: 'This Russian soldier is a girl.'

"This happened in the year 1914.

"We found out that the girl was the betrothed of a Russian officer, and fought side by side with him throughout the campaign, until killed by a shot in the breast. The officer was taken prisoner. I buried her myself that same day…"

In order to make clear what happened when I crossed the German border for the last time, I should explain that I now had with me several trophies which I had obtained with great difficulty and was correspondingly anxious to bring home. Among them was a German private's helmet and an original Iron Cross of the second degree. The marking on the temple band of the helmet said, "48th Regiment, 4th Army Corps, Company 7, No. 57, 1909-1914,"—meaning that the owner started service in 1909 and the helmet was issued to him in 1914. It is believed it belonged to a soldier who was either wounded or killed outside of Antwerp. The Iron Cross has on it: "1870" (when the order was started), and the letter "F" (Friedrich), and the date of its issuance. I should add that I did not rob a dead or dying soldier of these trophies, but I was asked not to show them in either Belgium or England, nor to state how I came by them. And I have kept my promise.

I had also a fragment of shrapnel casing from a 32 cm. shell—the only bomb which hit the Antwerp Cathedral during the German attack. It was given to me by Mr. Edward Eyre Hunt, who picked it up on the morning of the German entry. There were also some Belgian bullet clips and a bit of shrapnel picked up near the spot where I was knocked down by the concussion of a bursting shell on that same morning.

When I reached Bentheim we were put through the usual search by the border patrol and military officials of the Zollamt. I had pinned the Iron Cross to my undershirt, but the helmet was a bit bulky for such treatment.

"Take it out!" roared the officer who discovered the headgear wrapped in a sweater in my rucksack. "Dass ist str-r-reng ver-r-rboten!"

When I explained that I had come by it honestly, and wanted to take it home, he burst into a passion. The fact that I showed a letter from Von Bernstorff and explained that I was known in the Foreign Office in Berlin made no impression whatsoever. The officer said that if the owner was dead, the helmet could not even go to his family. It was government property and should return, therefore, to the commissary department. At all events, it must not leave the Empire.

I missed my train and was kept in Bentheim overnight. In the morning I again tried persuasion, but without success. As it was now a question of myself or the helmet, I decided to get myself home. I went back once more, and as a final chance put up this proposition to my officer. I showed my credentials and explained that I was going to The Hague. Would he in the mean time put my name on the helmet, and if within forty-eight hours he received a wire both from the Foreign Office in Berlin and The Hague Legation, would he send the helmet after me? He glared at me for a moment. Yes, he said, he would.

At The Hague I immediately visited the German Legation and told them of the customs officer's promise.

From bitter experience I realized that in war-time out of sight is lost, so far as baggage is concerned. Consequently I had given up all hope of my trophy. A week later, when I happened to be in Dr. van Dyke's study, I noticed a conical-shaped object resting on one of the secretary's desks. There, on top of a pile of letters, with "Herr Horace Green" scribbled in German script on a piece of paper pinned to the green-gray service covering, lay my dented, battered, and long-lost German private's helmet!

Simply because the fiery customs officer had given his word, the German Legation at The Hague had telegraphed to Bentheim and also, I take it, to Excellency von Mumm at Berlin; and the customs officials had shipped the helmet to the Dutch capital, where the German Legation, obedient to promise, had turned it over to the American Legation for delivery to me. The whole proceeding seemed typical of the overbearing gruffness, the systematic attention to detail, and at the same time the thoroughgoing honesty of the German character.

So I tucked the helmet under my arm, and, saying good-bye to Dr. van Dyke and Mr. Langhome, who had made my stay at The Hague so pleasant, I crossed the mine-strewn English Channel for Piccadilly Circus.

Two weeks later I was aboard the Red Star liner Lapland, driven one hundred miles out of her course through fear of German war craft, yet pounding along through a thick fog and hopefully headed in the general direction of the good old Statue of Liberty.

Appendix: Atrocities

I gained the impressions given below and compiled many of the instances on the now threadbare subject of atrocities during the time that I was in the war zone. The opinions will not meet with favor in this country, particularly at present, when we seem on the point of breaking diplomatic relations with Germany.

Nevertheless, I think these notes present a point of view which ought to be known, if only for the purpose of showing the other side of the shield—and of checking, to some extent, the nursery tales in regard to personal atrocities, which become more fanciful the farther they are told from the scene of reported occurrence. After the horrible Lusitania crime and other evidences of German Schrecklichkeit for which there can be no justification, it is hard for Americans to reason fairly in questions involving Teutonic methods of warfare. I am therefore appending the notes in spite of a rather careful study of the Bryce Report on German atrocities in Belgium. They are, of course, to be taken into consideration merely as the evidence of what one man happened to see or as was often more the case, not to see.

In order that there may be no misunderstanding, it is well to define the meaning of the word "atrocity."

I suppose all will agree with me that the term does not include what may be called the necessary horrors of war—such as hunger and poverty resulting from the destruction of homes and loss of livelihood, the suffering of refugees driven by necessity from captured towns, starvation through no fault of the invader, the accidental wounding of noncombatant peasants, farmers, etc. For the present purpose the word is intended to include all cases of unnecessary, unprovoked personal cruelty, as well as, of course, the outraging of women. Such acts, for example, as the reported gouging-out of the eyes of prisoners, cutting off the wrists of children, the alleged stabbing of old women, cutting off the wrists and ears of nurses, and the more refined cruelties of which I have heard reports, are, it goes without saying, atrocities. Let us examine one or two of these.

Near Osnabruck, Germany, an American visitor, pacing up and down a railroad siding early one morning, chewing a mouthful of stale sausage meat between thick crusts of rye bread, heard a particular cruelty story which may be used here as an example. It was told by an army surgeon with whom he was having his peripatetic breakfast. On the track alongside stood a so-called Red Cross train, consisting of a combination of well-equipped hospital coaches with their triple rows of berths slung one above the other as in a sleeper; attached in the rear were a few coal carriages and freight trucks. This train was waiting for the outbound traffic to pass by. You see, the outbound traffic consisted of fresh troops, being rushed to the front in one of those quick transcontinental shifts which have played so important a part in German strategy. But the eastbound train carried only wounded and dying on their way back home. So, of course, the hospital cars must wait as long as necessary, since they had no right or standing in the ruthless game called war.

In the cheerless interior of one of these freight cars (much the same kind of car as that in which we were confined during the trip from Brussels to Aix—apparently used as a horse-stall on the previous trip, and with no bedding beyond a damp pile of straw in one corner) the American noticed a young German private. This particular fellow was not wounded. He wore no bandages; he was the only occupant of the horse-stall; and he paced up and down the boards, muttering, muttering, continually muttering to himself. Now and then he snatched up a musket, went through the form of fixing a bayonet, and again and again lunged savagely at the wall of the car.

The Red Cross surgeon to whom the American went for information dismissed the matter casually by merely tapping his forehead with his index finger.

"Just one of those insane cases," he said.

Later in the day on better acquaintance the surgeon explained the matter in this fashion: —

"The fellow was quartered in a village near Lille, doing sentry duty on a house occupied by German officers. There was an uprising of citizens. From across the way native franc-tireurs fired shots into the house, killing one officer and wounding a second. Tracing the firing across the street, the remaining officers entered a bakery-shop where they found several men and a woman, all armed. They ordered the men to be shot. The woman had in her hand a revolver with one of the cartridge chambers empty. The German lieutenant saw that she was about to become a mother. He then explained the gravity of her offense, told her that she was practically guilty of murder, and took away her weapon. But under the circumstances he ordered her released instead of being shot. He turned his back and walked away about five paces. Suddenly the woman snatched another revolver from behind the counter and fired point-blank. As he fell, the officer called out to his orderly, 'Bayonet the woman.'

"The sentry did what he was ordered, but, you see, it has affected the poor fellow's mind."

This story, along with a few others, I have picked out from hundreds of atrocity tales which I heard during four months spent in England, Belgium, Germany, and Holland. It will serve as an example, not only because it has the earmarks of truth, — having been told in an offhand way merely as an explanation of the private's insanity, — but because it is typical of the kind of incident which in the telling is, nine times out of ten, twisted into atrocious and wholly unrecognizable form.

Under the law of military reprisal was there justification for the death of this woman? Was the dying officer guilty of barbarian conduct? And did the private, ordered against his will to perform an act whose memory drove him insane, commit an atrocity? Without answering the question, let us consider for a moment how that particular anecdote would be told by a Belgian partisan. In my wanderings through Termonde, Liege, and Louvain, I heard tales—unspeakable and on their face utterly unbelievable—of which this kind of thing must have been the foundation.

When the body of this woman was found, let us say, by French peasants returning to their ruined homes, think how the horrible fact would be seized, without whatsoever there was of justification! How the British and French papers would describe that mutilated form! Think of the effect of a two-column word-picture of the wanton sack and ruin of the town, the shooting of its helpless citizens, and the description of that mangled body sacrified to the Huns! Think how the fact would be clutched by fear-crazed inhabitants, would be bandied from mouth to mouth, distorted and dressed up to suit a partisan press, and "twisted by knaves to make a trap for fools"!

One of the first atrocity accounts which I heard in Belgium, as well as one of the most persistent, had to do with scores of children whose wrists had been cut by the Kaiser's troops. Hundreds of them were reported to be in Belgium and Dutch hospitals or in the care of relief committees. The gossip was so prevalent and in some instances so specific that I had high hopes of tracking down and seeing, with my own eyes, an instance. In each case which I heard abroad, my informant's husband or brother or best friend had seen the children; but somehow or other it was never arranged that I could see one of them myself. This type of cruelty was so widely talked about that in plenty of cases the German soldiers believed that some of their men had committed these crimes. One of them told me that he understood that near Tirlemont the wrists of several young children had been cut. He said that thirty or forty children and peasants had fired on and killed German troops marching through a neighboring village. A squad was sent to round up the offenders, all of whom were found armed. Instead of killing the snipers, whose age was between ten and seventeen, the surgeons were ordered to slice the tendons of the wrist so that the noncombatants should be prevented from holding a gun or using a knife.

Soon after my ship, the Lapland, docked in America, I heard a case of whose verity, owing to the source from which it came, I had no doubt. The refugee in question, according to my informant, was an English nurse, and lay with both wrists cut off at a well-known New York hospital on Madison Avenue. She had been in Brussels at the time of the German entry, and, being willing to work for the sake of humanity wheresoever there were sick to care for, she had nursed wounded German officers. Eventually, with a handful of English nurses still remaining in Brussels, she had been deported to Holland, because it was feared that German secrets were leaking out in letters sent by these English nurses. This latter part coincided so precisely with the facts which during my stay in Brussels I had found to be true, that I had no doubt of the whole business. On recovery the nurse was to exhibit herself and lecture for Red Cross funds. I was told this in strict confidence and I was to see and talk to the handless lady on condition that the "story" should not reach the press. I agreed. But to my bitter disappointment the — —- Hospital had never heard of the woman. My informant then confessed that his informant had made a mistake in the name of the hospital. I offered four persons ten dollars each to trace the matter to its source, the final result being a telephone call from my informant saying that an English lawyer now in New York stated that to the best of his belief there was "some such person in a hospital somewhere in New Jersey."

Merely for what they may be worth, and not in any sense as conclusive, I mention the cases which came to my attention. During a month spent in that part of Belgium where the most savage of the atrocities were reported,—a month devoted to a diligent search for the truth,—I could run down only two instances where the facts were proved, and where taken all in all and looked at from both sides they constituted an atrocity. I lived in an atmosphere of popular apprehension frequently amounting to terror. A friend of mine saw children throw up their hands in terror and fall down on their knees before a squad of German Uhlans who suddenly dashed into a village near Vilvorde. The incident does not prove that Uhlans are in the habit of acting atrociously; it does prove the popular fear of them. Near the same town I investigated the case of a peaceful villager, reported in the current conversation of the story to have had his ears cut off and to have been finished off with a half-dozen bayonet wounds. This I got at first hand from the man who had seen the body. I asked him how he knew the man had been bayoneted by Germans. My informant said that he himself was running from the village, where a skirmish was going on between a regiment of the enemy (Germans) and Belgian carabineers, that he was racing for his life through a rain of bullets, etc., etc., and that under fire of sharpshooters he stumbled across this body. He did not know the man was dead; but the case interested him. So later he went back (still under fire of the sharpshooters) and counted the number of holes in the man's shirt; there were six, he told me, and he was sure from the shape of the holes that they were the result of bayonets, not bullets.

At one time when driving from Ghent toward Brussels with Julius Van Hee, the acting Consul-General of the United States at Ghent, we passed a little hillock of ground upon which was a small square slab of stone, topped by a pair of sticks—hardly more than sticks—in the shape of a cross. There was a yarn floating around the neighborhood, which had almost crystallized into legend, that this was the fresh grave of a child murdered by the Germans because it refused to salute. They said the feet had been cut off and the boy was left to bleed to death. Conceivably the story was true. We did not stop, for we could not carry the investigation to the point of digging up a fresh grave.

On the evening previous Van Hee had gone over to his office to lock up preparatory to our early start for Brussels. A woman of Louvain stood on the doorstep. How on earth she had ever got back to Ghent, neither Van Hee nor Luther, who was in Van Hee's office and who told me the story, could make out from her incoherent words. She had been torn from her family, driven from house and home with a mob of wretched women, and shipped into Cologne, Germany. She was almost starved; several others went mad for lack of water. She now believed herself a widow. Between tears and hysterics she told how soldiers had entered her house, how two of them had held her husband against the wall at the point of a revolver, while "several" others in succession violated her before her husband's eyes!!

These stories are not pleasant. But in seeking the real facts one cannot work with kid gloves. Of the hundreds I have heard I have mentioned a few of those which show the kind of thing believed to have occurred in the ravaged country. Of all those which I heard, the last mentioned and the one at the head of this chapter—for which there was justification—appeared to have the greatest probability of truth.

During the first rush of war the German system of destruction, and the doctrine of "awfulness," as I saw it applied to physical objects, was barbaric, relentless, and totally unjustified. At Louvain, Aerschot, and Termonde it was at its height. On the other hand, in the mind of an impartial student of the facts there cannot be the slightest doubt that at Louvain there was an organized attack on the invaders by snipers and franc-tireurs armed with knives, guns, revolvers of every description. A half-day spent en route from burning Antwerp with a Jesuit priest of Louvain and the testimony of several villagers would have convinced me of this, had I not already been convinced by the stories of other survivors.

The burning of villages is one matter, the outraging and torturing of women and children another. The truth of the former should not in any way convict a German officer, much less Private Johann Schmidt, of unprovoked personal cruelty.

There undoubtedly were, though I did not happen to see them, numerous cases of unprovoked cruelty and other evidences of barbarity that are bound to happen in any war of invasion. The fact that I, personally, did not happen to see them, and have found scarcely a non-partisan observer who did, is neither here nor there. I merely state the fact as one of the many bits of evidence which should be taken into consideration. I have no case for Prussian militarism in so far as applied to inanimate objects. The German system of destruction in the early part of the war was utterly without excuse or justification; the wreck and desolation, the hunger and suffering of the larger portion of Belgium are utterly beyond the comprehension of those who have not been there. Certainly words cannot convey the impression. The suffering, particularly during the weeks following the fall of Antwerp, was so awful and on so large a scale that the senses refused to grasp it. It has been said that in the Civil War Sheridan was commanded, in pushing up the Shenandoah Valley, to leave the countryside in such condition that a crow could not live on it. A sparrow could not have existed in many parts of Belgium.

At the same time it is true that because of the tortures endured by the Belgian people, because of the pain and horror of the war of invasion, much of it unavoidable, the American public, because its sentiment is so strongly anti-German, has been willing to believe anything of the race against whom runs its prejudice. Truly remarkable is the rapidity with which atrocity stories have been created and the relish with which they are swallowed by drawing-room gossips. Those who have seen the war do not find it necessary to talk about what does not exist. Mr. Arthur Ruhl, who has seen and carefully studied all sides of the war, applies the term "nursery tale" to the average atrocity story. Mr. Irvin Cobb, John T. McCutcheon, and others who have been on the ground also took them with a grain of salt. Curiously enough, the closer one got to the actual fight, the less bitter was the feeling between participants, the greater their respect for one another, and the less credulous their belief in the enemy's barbarity.

An American who was recently discharged from seven months' service with the British army tells me that during this time the only knowledge he had of personal atrocities was through the British and French newspapers. And there are well-known stories of opposing trenches so closely situated that the soldiers taught each other their respective national airs, and the choruses of their camp tunes.

To return to another form of alleged outrage, we have the ancient argument on the case of Rheims.

An interesting contribution to the testimony has been given by Cyril Brown, now special correspondent of the New York Times in Berlin. Brown made his way to the German army lines before Rheims, where, among others, he interviewed First Lieutenant Wengler, of the Heavy Artillery, commander of a battery which shelled the church spire, but known among his comrades as "the little friend of the Rheims Cathedral." According to Lieutenant Wengler two shots only struck the church spire (one from a fifteen centimeter howitzer, another from a twenty-one centimeter mortar) and this after French observers had used the tower for five days between September thirteenth and eighteenth. So sparing was this young "barbarian," in spite of provocative fire obviously directed from the French cathedral, that "the friend of the Rheims Cathedral" stuck to him as a nickname.

In America Brown's statement provoked a storm of retort. Allied correspondents claimed that a dozen shots at least crashed through the roof, set the scaffolding ablaze, and that, at a time when Red Cross flags were floating from the tower and red crosses were painted on the roof, shells continued to devastate the beautiful interior, etc., etc. There has been a quantity of discussion back and forth as to the number of shots fired. Now, so far as the question of atrocity is concerned, though every one will regret the ruin of this noble work of art, I hold that it is not of the slightest importance whether there were fired two shells or seventeen or seventy-seven. The important and only question at issue is, whether the tower was used for observation purposes, or, in other words, was there military justification for its attempted destruction?

Military men, English as well as German, to whom I have talked, take it as a matter of course that the highest spot in any locality is used for observation. As an English officer in Antwerp put it, "If the French did not use the church tower they are d — — —fools."

By way of guide and for sake of likely comparison I can state what I know did happen in two other cities: Termonde and Antwerp. In Chapter II of this book I have told how we made our way across the broken bridge at Termonde on the day of its second bombardment, and how that night word came to us of the manner in which the Belgians took revenge on the conquerors. I told how staff officers, entering with a scouting party at the head of a German column, mounted the only remaining spire in the town. With a few well-directed shots from their concealed batteries west of the river, the Belgians destroyed the tower and killed the officers. The Belgians took no little pride in their marksmanship on that occasion, and boasted freely of it. In this case, the use, and therefore the destruction, of the observation-post was looked upon by the Belgians as a natural and necessary instance of the work of war. As evidence, it is rather valuable because given unconsciously and without motive.

Likewise at Antwerp. In all probability the fact has never been appreciated that during the bombardment of this city,—the most important, from a military point of view, in Belgium,—the spire of the Notre Dame Cathedral was used as an outlook-station by the Belgian defenders, if not by both Belgians and English. On the inadvertent testimony of English themselves I know this to be true. On the second night of the Antwerp bombardment the Americans who had not left the city were gathered in the almost deserted Queen's Hotel along the water front. Some time during the evening, I don't remember just when, but it was while the British retreat was going on, an English lad called Lucien Arthur Jones burst in upon us. At no little risk he had dodged through the deserted streets and falling shells, much elated over the view of the enemy he had just got from the cathedral tower.

"I've had bully luck," he confided to me, after I had done him a noble service (i.e., lent him a safety razor). "Belgian signal officers took me up to the tower, where they can see everything the Germans are doing."

The following is taken from his account—an Englishman's account— printed in the London Chronicle, and copied in the New York Times, Tribune, and other papers:—

"I now return to the events of Thursday. At 12.30 o'clock in the afternoon, when the bombardment had already lasted over twelve hours, through the courtesy of a Belgian officer, I was able to ascend to the roof of the cathedral, and from that point of vantage I looked down upon the scene in the city. I could just discern through my glasses dimly in the distance the instruments of culture of the attacking German forces ruthlessly pounding at the city and creeping nearer to it in the dark. At that moment I should say the enemy's front line was within four miles of Antwerp.

"From my elevated position I had an excellent view also of the great oil tanks on the opposite side of the Scheldt. They had been set on fire by four bombs from a German Taube, and a huge, thick volume of black smoke was ascending two hundred feet into the air. The oil had been burning furiously for several hours, and the whole neighborhood was enveloped in a mist of smoke.

"After watching for some considerable time the panorama of destruction that lay unrolled all around me, I came down from my post of observation on the cathedral roof, and at the very moment I reached the street a 28- centimeter shell struck a confectioner's shop between the Place Verte and the Place de Meir. It was one of these high-explosive shells, and the shop, a wooden structure, immediately burst into flames."

Recapitulation

The destruction of towns and villages, and the vengeance against inanimate objects shown in the German march through Belgium was barbaric. It was provoked by organized resistance on the part of Belgian franc-tireurs, and by shooting from behind shutters, etc., and other attacks by citizens of the invaded country. The Germans, though truthful in the statement of the causes, inflicted punishment out of all proportion to the crime.

The reports of unprovoked personal atrocities, it is nevertheless true, have been hideously exaggerated. Wherever one real atrocity has occurred, it has been multigraphed into a hundred cases. Each, with clever variation in detail, is reported as occurring to a relative or close friend of the teller. For campaign purposes, and particularly in England for the sake of stimulating recruiting, a partisan press has helped along the concoction of lies.

In every war of invasion there is bound to occur a certain amount of plunder and rapine. The German system of reprisal is relentless; but the German private as an individual is no more barbaric than his brother in the French, the British, or the Belgian trenches.

The End